"It is a pleasure to endorse Tom's Book as he has made the topic so accessible to his readers. And doing so through the experience of an ED, it would be hard not to relate to Sue and Second Chance. Tom reminds us that our issues appear to revolve around program or resource development but are usually embedded in board and organizational development. Tom has provided many tools and techniques for digging deeper, that can be accomplished in a non-threatening way."

David M. McGowan, CFRE
President, The Dupage Community Foundation

W9-BSD-934

ISBN-13:978-0692366899
ISBN-10: 069236689X

ACCLAIM FOR BREAK THROUGH

"Tom Okarma knows where we all have been! A creative, practical, highly relevant book that will advance any nonprofit, but especially those in the early stages of organizational development. Every reader will find takeaways that work because Tom captures so many best practices."

Robert C. Andringa
Ph. D. Author and Governance expert; President Emeritus of the Council for Christian Colleges & Universities

"Tom Okarma is a non-profit organizational (NPO) genius. He brings time-tested excellent practices in one hand and in the other he offers the skillful patience to help you grow your impact and mission. In this book, Tom Okarma gets to the heart of the issues for NPOs trying to grow to the next level. If you don't immediately identify with book's main character and the problems she faces, chances are you soon will. Read this book, then buy a copy for every CEO and board member of a NPO you know!"

CH Dyer
President and CEO, Bright Hope International

"When an airplane stalls, effectiveness is reduced. When nonprofits stall, likewise, effectiveness wanes. In Break Through the Ick Factors, Tom Okarma insightfully identifies some of the most critical factors which often impede progress of nonprofits. Then, he insightfully identifies solutions for these common challenges. Leaders will find this book very useful in maximizing a nonprofit's potential."

Dan Busby
President, ECFA

"Strong leaders are willing to take a hard look in the mirror when it comes to evaluating how effectively they are leading their organizations and boards. Tom Okarma enables leaders to see the good, bad, and in this case the icky, about what is working and what may not be working in their leadership. The case study illustrates the issues and the potential that exists on the other side of breakthrough. This book will shift your thinking and focus you for higher impact for greater return."

Tami Heim

President & CEO, Christian Leadership Alliance

"It's rarely the passion that the leader of a non-profit lacks, but the strategy and the right people around them to implement the calling they have been given. Tom addresses the needs of a non-profit accurately and gives solutions in a simple and repetitive format that causes one to feel they are sitting at the table with him throughout the book. Well done, Tom!"

Annette Forster

Partnerships - Illinois Director, Kids Hope USA

"There are many books written for business leaders, but rarely do those books address the unique leadership issues encountered by non-profits, until now. Break Through is a must read for anyone serving in non-profit leadership! All of the "icky" topics non-profit leaders tend to avoid rather than face head-on are addressed in this book. Tom not only addresses those issues, but gives direct advice and practical resources to resolve them. Do yourself and your non-profit a favor; read this book and implement the resources it gives!"

Christa March

President, Teen Mother Choices International

BREAK THROUGH

THE ICK FACTORS

of nonprofit leadership

discover your organization's true potential

TOM OKARMA

CONTENTS

CONTENTS

PREFACE (From Tom)

Break Through is a story drawn from my personal experiences working and volunteering in the nonprofit community. While there is no Second Chance nonprofit agency in real life, I have worked with a number of nonprofits dealing with similar challenges. I have created this story to illustrate some of the most common issues and problems facing many nonprofits every day and hopefully shed some light on how to solve them.

These problems and issues can paralyze a leader or board if not handled well. They show up in the board room, in the organization's leadership, and in its operations. These are the challenges that keep nonprofits from getting to the next level and making a more significant impact. I call these challenges **ICK FACTORS** and you may recognize a few of them in your own agency.

ICK FACTORS can be problems, situations, or uncomfortable "people issues" that can make nonprofit leadership a bigger challenge than it needs to be. Some **ICK FACTORS** may not look like problems at first but eventually, by avoiding them, delaying their handling, or choosing the wrong strategy, they can cause huge headaches, friction, and even more problems down the road.

I hope you will find the suggestions in this book helpful and effective. I know they have worked elsewhere and I am confident they will help you.

I know nonprofit leadership can be complicated and you already have so much on your plate. Between fundraising, managing your board, staff and volunteers, and stretching your dollars farther, you have plenty to keep you busy.

I wrote this book to help you, the nonprofit leader and board member, face these problems head-on so you can focus on your important mission-critical work and not get bogged down in unnecessary drama and energy-draining problems. My goal is to equip you with ideas and tools to help you minimize or even avoid certain problems so you can lead your agency to do more, make a greater impact, and help more people.

These problems are solvable—some easier than others, for sure—but I want to help you see that these **ICK FACTORS** are not as difficult to face as they may at first appear.

Whether your agency is faith-based or secular, serving in the areas of social services, addictions, justice and equality, or otherwise, small or large, the issues that arise in this story–the **ICK FACTORS** of nonprofit leadership–can exist in virtually all of them.

The problems I suggest in the story are real and I have faced nearly all of them, in either the business world or nonprofit world, or both. My goal is to outline real-life nonprofit problems and suggest, or perhaps reaffirm in your own mind, solutions, to address those problems and issues you face every day.

Throughout the book I'll be pointing out these **ICK FACTORS** and offering solutions. Each **ICK FACTOR** will appear in the text as [**FACTOR #**].

In Part 2 of the book, you will find a complete list of each of the **ICK FACTORS** along with suggestions for how to overcome these challenges. As you are reading, you'll be invited to download a variety of resources from the book website www.ickfactors.com, to help you apply real solutions to the particular problem.

There are numerous challenges that face the nonprofit leader. Break Through focuses on the most critical areas, the **ICK FACTORS,** which if overcome, have the greatest potential to impact your organization in the biggest way.

I invite you to join me now and follow Sue, the hardworking Founder, Board Chair, and Executive Director of Second Chance, as she tells her story about what she did to break through her challenges and conquer the **ICK FACTORS** of nonprofit leadership.

- Tom Okarma

Part 1:
The Story

1

THE REASON WHY

It was a chilly Tuesday morning as I made my way through the front door of Second Chance. I was immediately drawn to a pair of bright blue eyes, peeking out from under a worn baseball cap. That little boy's eyes were so haunting, and he wasn't even looking at me, he was staring up at his mother next to him. I will never forget the look in those eyes... they said so much. They were full of worry, fear, and doubt. I just had to say hello and talk to him.

His name was Joey, and the way he looked at his mother tore into me like nothing before. They were relatively new clients of ours, and I'd only seen them a couple times before. I could only imagine how the mother felt, unable to help support her family and having to come to a food pantry for help. Though only a young child, I think Joey could tell something was wrong, he just didn't know what.

I quickly learned Joey was 7 years old and had two sisters, both younger. His dad worked part-time in a hardware store and was gone a lot looking for other jobs. Joey loved to draw and promised to draw a picture of his family for me.

The young boy loved sports and was doing "ok" in school, although he admitted he'd rather play than do homework. Joey knew nothing about recessions, being out of work, or running through one's savings, but he knew his mom wasn't herself. He couldn't remember the last time she smiled or played with him. He was just an average little boy trying to grow up in a tough situation.

I spoke briefly with his mother and learned she and his father had been out of full-time work for quite a while and were no longer able to provide for the family. It was obvious this was taking a huge toll on her.

Joey's dad was a contractor who had always made a decent living building homes, but after 8 years, when the economy took a down turn, he was laid off. The family had been working hard to make ends meet on their own, cutting here and there, with dad picking up side jobs when possible, and then dipping into their savings when necessary. But now they were no longer able to make ends meet.

They had tried to avoid having to go to a food pantry. She told me they tried everything else. All that was left was to come to Second Chance for help. I felt so bad for them.

I couldn't put myself in the mother's shoes but I certainly knew how badly I felt—alone, sad, and frustrated. I felt like a failure. I was no longer confident we would be able to meet the immediate needs of Joey and his family, and so many others like them. In the end we sent them home with much less food than they had hoped to get from us, and certainly much less than we normally gave to families of five.

Our entire staff—all the volunteers and I—had been working so hard to avoid running out of food and supplies but it felt like we were fighting a losing battle. The food pantry shelves had never been so low and the waiting lines stretched outside our doors every day. We just couldn't keep up with the growing demand. I spent much of my time on the phone to our retail donors trying to get additional donations, with limited success.

I felt awful! I had to do something to turn things around. There was so much need, so many people relying on Second Chance. This was my community and I had to do something!

Continuing to do my job as usual just wasn't working! Something had to change at Second Chance and as the Executive Director, I was the one who was supposed to have all the answers...

2

SUE'S STORY

I am the Founder and Executive Director of Second Chance Food Pantry & Clothing Closet, a six year old nonprofit dedicated to helping out-of-work and underemployed residents. I guess I've always had a passion to help those in need, so when I saw the number of unemployed people in our community growing I wanted to do something to help them.

I am married with two children, one in high school and one in college. Before I started Second Chance, my husband was a sales rep for a pharmaceutical company and frequently traveled on his job, while I worked at a local insurance agency. I spent ten years helping our clients by processing their auto and homeowners' claims with the insurance companies.

Eventually, as my husband moved up the ladder at work I became a stay-at-home mom— a wonderful opportunity while our kids were young—but it left me with a lot of free time as they grew older. That's when I realized how much I missed helping others. I had helped a lot of people while at the agency, and with time on my hands I had been looking for an opportunity to do something completely different.

§

Six years ago I decided to start a food pantry and clothing closet. I saw a need in our community, and I wanted to help those people. I believed everyone deserved a second chance. Things had gone well for about four years, we grew and I learned so much.

But two years ago our local economy took a significant hit and we started seeing many more people out of work and coming to Second Chance. It was the most people I'd ever seen. Our community was in trouble and the numbers just kept climbing.

We had always been able to help almost anyone who came to us. But now we were experiencing periodic shortages and were even forced to close at times, since we had little-to-no food available. Our finances were stretched to the limit and we were falling short of the resources we needed to do our job well.

The retail stores which had been so reliable in sending us donations of food, clothing and other personal items had begun carrying less inventory, due to the slowdown in their own businesses. That meant they had less and less overstock to donate to us.

We had to go back to our most generous and loyal donors so many extra times, I felt we were starting to experience donor fatigue. Our average gift started to decline and some of our most reliable donors were becoming less and less frequent in their giving.

As a result, more often than not, our food pantry cupboards were almost as bare as those of our clients. Over time, we had become their backstop in case they ran short of food or clothing, but over the past 6-12 months especially, we struggled to be that reliable resource they had come to count on.

This wasn't supposed to happen to a food pantry and clothing closet established to help those in need! I was in charge! I started this organization to help people! We were stretched to the limits, running out of food, and turning people away, and it all was happening under my watch!

3

THE SECOND CHANCE STORY

Our food pantry is located in Fortsville IL, about forty miles west of Chicago. For many years it was a thriving business area along the scenic Fox River. Fortsville is a medium-sized town and a good place to raise a family. Agriculture and manufacturing were its leading industries and they combined to make Fortsville an important business town in the region. But when the economy weakened, leading to a nationwide recession, all of Fortsville's manufacturers were hit extremely hard. It seemed like every week more people were being laid off.

Starting about a year ago—over a period of six months— three major local manufacturers closed down their operations altogether, forcing many people out of work and onto unemployment. Soon the entire town was feeling the pinch one way or the other, throwing the entire region into a recession of its own. A once thriving suburban community was now staggering and in trouble.

The state's unemployment programs provided some relief, and several regional nonprofits stepped in to help, but this slowdown was deep and real. It had also caused a domino effect. Businesses either declined or shut their doors as people stopped spending. Retailers, restaurants, and grocery stores, slowed down or closed due to a lack of business. It was clear to us that the town and all of the residents, were in for an extended period of adjustment and reinvention.

§

I'd always had a heart for those in need. It was my passion. I can't tell you just when this passion developed but I likely picked it up from my parents. They were very generous people, quite active in the local nonprofit and church communities. I really enjoyed helping people who needed an extra hand to get past some challenging times in life.

Six years ago, when Fortsville's unemployment rose to 9%, it just made sense to me, to start something like Second Chance. I wanted to provide the people in our community with food and clothing, but more importantly, with encouragement, respect, and an opportunity to stabilize their living situation. I felt all they needed was a way to help themselves get back on their feet. Second Chance's doors were open to anyone in the community needing our help.

§

When we started the organization I was fortunate enough to recruit and surround myself with five very kind-hearted and generous friends, I knew well and trusted. They were terrific volunteers and provided me with much needed support— financial and emotional. They were a tremendous help to me in launching Second Chance.

When I first created my Board of Directors I naturally asked them to join me. My board was composed of my husband, a close neighbor of ours, my sister, and two other close friends. They were excited to help me get things going. [**FACTOR 1**] Before long we received our 501(c)(3) status approval from the government and we were on our way.

ICK FACTOR 1: NON-STRATEGIC BOARD CANDIDATE SOURCING

For quite a while things went well. Everyone on the board did double duty both as a director and a volunteer. They had fun, helped a lot of people, and felt good about the way they were contributing to our community's well-being. Problems were few—often quite small and easy to handle—and relatively speaking, all was good.

Over time, like any growing and successful operation, Second Chance began facing new and more complicated issues— issues beyond the board's experience and skill. Decisions were increasingly deferred to me, and the board just rubber-stamped whatever recommendations I proposed.

Even though our directors loved serving at Second Chance, they were just not equipped [**FACTOR 1**] to handle and solve the kinds of problems we were facing. Problems like a lack of funding, decrease in in-kind donations, lack of marketing or social media programs, and inadequate facilities were just a few. As we grew we were becoming slow and bureaucratic, and we were losing our nimbleness.

ICK FACTOR 1: NON-STRATEGIC BOARD CANDIDATE SOURCING

Second Chance had always had an adequate supply of food, but now not only were we short on food, we were short of cash, too. We had nonperishable food supplies filling only two of our five shelving units. We rarely ever got that low on food! Too frequently we were worrying about where that next cash gift was coming from so we could just keep our heads above water.

On top of that, we were running out of space to serve our growing number of clients. We were experiencing a 20% year over year increase in clients coming to see us. Our twelve volunteers were being stretched to the max and I feared they were on the verge of burnout.

Second Chance was operating out of a packed 2,400 square-foot space in a local industrial center. Our space, which had been more than adequate our first 4+ years, was significantly less than what we needed to serve our clients today, and would certainly be even more inadequate in the not-to-distant future. Our current space included three small offices and a conference room, a separate food pantry area with a refrigerator and a freezer, a small clothing closet area, and a small reception/intake area.

§

When I started Second Chance I built it by going door-to-door asking for cash, food, and clothing donations from retailers, churches, friends and neighbors—anyone who would listen to me. I had found grant applications to be complicated and they took so long to complete I usually tried to avoid them. I just didn't have the time, or the data, those applications really required. But eventually I had started working to complete them on the weekends since our need was so great!

Over time, and almost entirely by myself, [**FACTOR 2, 3**] I was able to grow Second Chance to the point of annually raising about $300,000 in in-kind gifts from various retailers, churches, neighbors and friends. We also received $400,000 in cash donations from my husband and I, grants from local private donors, foundations, local governments, my friends, neighbors and family members, periodic mail solicitation campaigns, a few small fund-raising events each year and from some federally-subsidized food purchasing programs.

ICK FACTOR 2: NOT DELEGATING AUTHORITY, TASKS OR PROJECTS

ICK FACTOR 3: WEAK VOLUNTEER ORIENTATION AND MANAGEMENT

Eventually I was able to draw a salary of $25,000 a year as Executive Director—that is, when the money was there—and I was able to hire four part-time employees who were paid on an hourly basis. Their hours varied greatly depending on client need and Second Chance having the money to pay them.

As we got busier with more and more clients, our costs started going through the roof. I needed our staff more often and for longer hours, and we needed to purchase more food.

I was so grateful for our true heroes—our volunteers. We had about a dozen volunteers, really reliable "regulars" I could count on to show up and help. They were the backbone of the agency and I relied on them a great deal. They helped us stretch our dollars so we could spend more money on food.

I had a good friend from school, Bill, who was a CPA, and after our first year, I was able to talk him into handling the books for us at rock-bottom nonprofit prices, and to serve on the board as our treasurer. As we started to grow, the accounting and financial management area became more complicated and took up a lot of my time.

With Bill taking over those areas I could focus on what I knew best and what gave me the greatest joy. [**FACTOR 2**]. I loved working in the food pantry and clothing closet, chatting with clients, and making them feel important, respected, valued, and not forgotten. I also spent much of my time asking many businesses and community groups—churches, service organizations, and similar—for financial or in-kind help.

ICK FACTOR 2: NOT DELEGATING AUTHORITY, TASKS OR PROJECTS

I was completely committed to Second Chance, and our clients—just ask my husband and kids. I loved giving presentations to any civic group, church spoke, whatever, about our work, wherever I could arrange a presentation.

I think my enthusiasm is why I always had an adequate number of well-meaning, dedicated volunteers to serve our clients, and enough food supplies and clothing items for them to distribute.

I've always had great volunteers; they've been like family to me. I started with just four and now that number had tripled.

In truth, I could probably use several more right now to ease the burden. Each of them has always respected our mission and shared my passion. They are motivated to give back to the community and Second Chance has always been there to give them that opportunity.

I tried hard to show them my appreciation and make it easy for them to contribute their time and talents to make a difference and feel good about themselves. But I was often so busy I took them for granted and let them just handle things on their own. [**FACTOR 3, 10**]

ICK FACTOR 3: WEAK VOLUNTEER ORIENTATION AND MANAGEMENT

ICK FACTOR 10: INEFFECTIVE OR MISSING ANNUAL PERFORMANCE REVIEWS, FEEDBACK, AND ASSESSMENTS

With the help of my dear husband and our teenage daughter, I managed to create and send out an email newsletter, though it was a bit irregular in timing. I had so much on my plate we just did it as time allowed. [**FACTOR 2**]

It generated donations each time it was sent but I knew we could be using it more effectively to raise money, in-kind donations and increase community awareness. I was just too busy to put more time into it. [**FACTOR 2**]

ICK FACTOR 2: NOT DELEGATING AUTHORITY, TASKS OR PROJECTS

21

I loved telling the Second Chance story and always looked for ways to reconnect with our current and any would-be donors when I was in their neighborhoods. I would tell them about the kinds of challenges our clients faced—job loss, medical expenses, even just getting around town—especially when their cars needed costly repairs.

One donor told me my passion and enthusiasm were contagious to anyone around me. I had never considered myself "good" at marketing or sales. I figured if I just told our clients' stories in compelling ways, people would join me and help out. Up until now, my approach worked pretty well and we always had enough money and food.

All in all, the agency had done an incredible job providing resources for so many people who needed help. In their eyes, Second Chance had become a life saver.

§

Until the last year or so, things had been going along fairly well and Second Chance was able to keep up with the needs of the community. Granted, from time to time we would run short of some food products, personal items, and some specific clothing items in the closet, like children's diapers, but never like this…

I had always worked hard, even donating our own money and much of my time to create Second Chance and get it off the ground. Even today, I was often the first one in the office in the morning—when I wasn't presenting somewhere—and was usually the last to leave at night.

On occasion in the past, we might have just run low on food during summer months and a little short of money from time to time. But now, this steady increase in demand for help was beginning to take its toll on us, our grocery store and other retail suppliers, and our cash donors. I was concerned we might not be able to provide for the needs of our clients and even more concerned that we might have to shut our doors.

No matter how well I budgeted or how hard I worked at raising money and managing our expenses, I learned two things for sure. Income was always hard to come by and costs were always on the rise. I was constantly searching out more sources of funding, but the expenses, just seemed to show up on their own.

Over the last 12 months things just kept getting worse. More and more people came to us for help and I found myself busier than ever. Second Chance was seeing a 20% year-over-year increase in new clients, and existing clients were continuing to use our services about three months longer, since they couldn't get back on their own as quickly as before. It was not unusual for us to have a line of people standing outside our doors and stretching all the way around the corner, sometimes with people standing in the rain.

I always wanted every client to experience as personal and respectful a visit to Second Chance as possible. No ID numbers here! Everyone was a human being deserving of respect and courtesy. I even helped our intake volunteers at times, so we didn't have to rush people through the process.

I probably could have drafted some of our occasional volunteers to pitch in and donate some extra time with us, but

I felt as the leader I had to be there. I thought finding others to do something would just take longer than simply doing it myself, so I would just jump in and get to work. [**FACTOR 2**]

ICK FACTOR 2: NOT DELEGATING AUTHORITY, TASKS OR PROJECTS

Eventually, things just started piling up and I began to fall seriously behind in my duties. Days turned into weeks, and weeks into months, and before I knew it, I was working at warp speed, doing just about anything that needed to be done. If there was a gap somewhere, I tried to fill it. No one could go home without food or clothing. I just would not allow it.

My situation was like the proverbial frog sitting in the pot of water, slowly heating up. I didn't notice how the pace of things had picked up until one evening I went home and crashed. I was tired, worn out and overwhelmed. Heck I was burned out. Sadly, so were many of my donors, staff, and volunteers. [**FACTOR 3, 10**]

ICK FACTOR 3: WEAK VOLUNTEER ORIENTATION AND MANAGEMENT

ICK FACTOR 10: INEFFECTIVE OR MISSING ANNUAL PERFORMANCE REVIEWS, FEEDBACK, AND ASSESSMENTS

§

I continued doing the best I could by putting in additional time to meet the growing need, and working even harder. I felt I couldn't really ask others to take on more work if I didn't take on more myself. **[FACTOR 2]** But one can only keep all the plates spinning for so long.

ICK FACTOR 2: NOT DELEGATING AUTHORITY, TASKS OR PROJECTS

In the past, I was usually able to solve our problems by working harder or putting in more hours, at least in the short term. But now all those extra hours and extra effort were taking their toll on me personally. The worst part of it was we were barely putting a dent in the backlog of clients looking for help. We were still serving everyone but we had begun to cut back on how much food we gave them. Rationing! I could not believe it!

Eventually I realized I had seriously over-scheduled myself and had completely lost any sense of work-life balance. On top of that, our income was not keeping pace with the increased demand.

All the pressure and hard work of trying to keep up had been squeezing the joy and passion out of me. I began to question myself. Can I do this? Is this too much for me? How could something like Second Chance, which seemed so right for our community, turn into something so wrong, burdensome, and heavy? What happened? And, scarier yet, if I was feeling this way, what about our volunteers and staff? They must be at the end of their ropes, too. Would they stick with me through all this? Could I lose them?

My passion remained as strong as ever but I had to admit I had hit a wall. I was burned out! Although I still had my strong commitment to our community, I finally realized things could not go on this way any longer. Something had to be done. As I left the office for the day, I decided to discuss this with the board at the next meeting that night. Something had to give. [**FACTOR 4**]

ICK FACTOR 4: POOR COMMUNICATION

I.F.

ICK FACTORS — CHAPTER 3

Following are the ICK FACTORS specifically mentioned in the chapter. For a complete listing of ICK FACTORS, along with suggestions for how to Break Through these challenges and other helpful resources, please visit section two of the book.

1. NON-STRATEGIC BOARD CANDIDATE SOURCING

2. NOT DELEGATING AUTHORITY, TASKS OR PROJECTS

3. WEAK VOLUNTEER ORIENTATION AND MANAGEMENT

4. POOR COMMUNICATION

10. INEFFECTIVE OR MISSING ANNUAL PERFORMANCE REVIEWS, FEEDBACK, AND ASSESSMENTS

4

THE BOARD MEETING

We always held our board meetings at 7:00 p.m, in the conference room, since it was pretty quiet around Second Chance in the evening. Clients, volunteers, and staff were usually gone by then.

Back in the early days I held a few of our board meetings in the back section of a local restaurant. I thought providing dinner was a good way to show my appreciation to the directors for their time and commitment. But over time that proved to be too distracting, and while the food was good, the meetings were terribly unproductive and basically a waste of time. Usually, I ended up taking on almost every task that came out of the meeting myself. [**FACTOR 1**]

ICK FACTOR 1: NON-STRATEGIC BOARD CANDIDATE SOURCING

The run-up to tonight's meeting went about the same as always. First I'd call each director to remind him or her of the meeting. [**FACTOR 5**] Then I'd pick up coffee, a few mini-scones (cranberry-orange, this time) some soft drinks and a few other snacks for the board as I drove to the meeting.

ICK FACTOR 5: A CULTURE WITHOUT A SENSE OF RESPONSIBILITY AND ACCOUNTABILITY

Once I got there, I'd make copies of various reports in case someone inevitably forgot his or her copy. Then I'd spend a few extra minutes cleaning up the conference room so it was ready for our board meeting since our volunteers and staff often ate lunch there.

The directors began strolling in just before 7:00 p.m, with the last one arriving around 7:20 p.m., but it was nearly 7:30 p.m. before everyone was settled in, with copies of the reports and handouts in front of them **[FACTOR 5].**

As Board Chair I finally called the meeting to order almost 30 minutes late–just like always. **[FACTOR 5]**

ICK FACTOR 5: A CULTURE WITHOUT A SENSE OF RESPONSIBILITY AND ACCOUNTABILITY

The first item on our agenda tonight was the Treasurer's report. I asked Bill to take everyone through the numbers and explain where Second Chance stood financially.

As he began, it soon became apparent no one had read the report in advance. For the next ten minutes I just sat there while everyone played catch up with the agenda and reports. **[FACTOR 5, 6]**

ICK FACTOR 5: A CULTURE WITHOUT A SENSE OF RESPONSIBILITY AND ACCOUNTABILITY

I restarted the meeting closer to 8:00 p.m. and began working through my agenda again.

Bill began a second time. "On the revenue side, we are running below budget again this month as well as for the quarter. In addition, our expenses have increased recently because food donations haven't kept pace with the demand we're experiencing due to our growing number of clients. We've had to purchase additional food and personal items for distribution. We've also had to spend some money on a few unanticipated repairs around the the office and food pantry. Our expenses are currently running over budget by about 15%."

"Thanks Bill," I nodded. "Just so you all are aware, I've been busy reaching out to several new grocery stores and retailers trying to fill this supply vs. demand gap with only limited results. Most of the stores I've approached aren't yet regular donors. I asked about their ability and willingness to donate food, clothing, and other personal items and they've responded, more or less. They are now donating some items, but not nearly in the quantities I had hoped for, or asked of them.

Unfortunately, I've pretty much exhausted all my current warm leads for additional resources or donations so I am not sure where I go from here."

I had hoped to stir up the board, maybe rock their world a bit, so they would feel what I felt every day in the food pantry. I told them my story about meeting Joey earlier and how the food pantry was almost empty. I showed them the picture Joey drew of his family for me, but they mostly just nodded and smiled sympathetically.

"Joey's family isn't the only hungry one in our community, just one of the most touching cases. We've seen so many new faces and families arriving lately— the single mom who lost her job because her car broke down and she couldn't get to work; the retired couple whose medicine was so expensive that they occasionally had to use the food pantry just to get through the month. These people desperately need us but we're falling short."

My point to the board was that we were facing an extremely serious food and cash shortage. It was a situation that was only getting worse, maybe even approaching crisis level, and we probably wouldn't be able to serve our clients much longer unless we took some kind of significant action.

"I really need your help in solving this problem! Does anyone have any suggestions on how you could pitch in?" [**FACTOR 6, 7**]

ICK FACTOR 6: DISENGAGED BOARD OR INDIVIDUAL DIRECTORS

ICK FACTOR 7: BOARD MEMBERS WHO DON'T DELIVER

The board remained silent for a bit, but then one director pointed out it was still early in the fiscal year. She thought these financial results might still be turned around by squeezing a little more revenue out of one or two of the upcoming fundraising events and carefully managing those repair expenses for the rest of the year. She also suggested that another mailing to donors asking for emergency help might be in order.

Definitely not what I wanted to hear but I said nothing and did my best to hide my frustration. Plodding ahead, I asked for other ideas on increasing revenue in case the upcoming events did not bring in as much as hoped.

After a long silence my sister eventually spoke up. "Sue, you do a great job running Second Chance, turning over every leaf looking for contributions and help. All of us on the board trust you to keep a watchful eye on the numbers and to do whatever you must do in the interim as we go through this rough patch. I suggest we all look at this again in 30 days at our next board meeting. I think this food shortage is just a little blip, a short term aberration, and things will get better by our next meeting."

I wanted to scream, but held my tongue. [**FACTOR 4**]

ICK FACTOR 4: POOR COMMUNICATION

No one had any other meaningful comments to add about the state of our food pantry or the treasurer's report itself. The report was approved without any further discussion.

The next agenda item was a report from our facilities committee. I had formed this committee last year, before our current cash and donation crisis arose. We 'd had a space problem for a while and it needed to be addressed. Our increase in clients only made this problem more pressing.

When I had formed this committee I told the board Second Chance had begun to run out of space and I was appalled that some of our clients had to wait outside our building when they arrived. We'd even begun using our conference room and private offices for intake purposes. At the busiest times there was little-to-no private space available. We had no discreet locations to meet with donors, clients or others who wanted to speak with us.

I had asked the committee to locate and evaluate other locations that might be suitable as the next site for Second Chance. We absolutely had to do something about our space constraints. We had long ago maxed-out our current location and no other space was available in the building we currently rented.

Our three offices and conference room were no longer sufficient to handle our growth and we really needed some private space to handle in-take interviews. I felt that no one should have to divulge their personal issues where others could overhear them.

The board agreed we needed more offices, more parking, more food pantry and clothing closet space, private intake cubicles, and a much larger waiting area. We had been growing significantly each of the last two years and it didn't look like it was going to slow down anytime soon.

One of my dearest friends Julie—the chair of the facilities committee—offered her report. "Well, I am embarrassed to report the committee hasn't met since the last board meeting, so I have no new details to report to the board at this time. [**FACTOR 5, 6**]

ICK FACTOR 5: A CULTURE WITHOUT A SENSE OF RESPONSIBILITY AND ACCOUNTABILITY

ICK FACTOR 6: DISENGAGED BOARD OR INDIVIDUAL DIRECTORS

But let me say this. After the one meeting we did have a few months ago we as a committee felt somewhat ill-equipped to address the expansion problem and wondered if you Sue, shouldn't just keep an eye out for additional locations on your own as you travel around town. We feel that since you understand the needs of Second Chance better than anyone else perhaps you should be the one doing the investigating."

My frustration grew. We'd just wasted three more months trying to address this problem without any help from the board or its facilities committee. But I held my tongue. I didn't want to disrupt things in a way that would only make matters worse. [**FACTOR 4**] How on earth could I add searching for a new location to everything I was already doing?

ICK FACTOR 4: POOR COMMUNICATION

Julie saw I was a bit off-put by her lack of report and tried to soothe things over by saying everyone on the committee trusted my judgment implicitly and would welcome my input and rely on my recommendations to ultimately resolve the space problem.

The board concurred and asked me to just keep thinking about our expansion and to keep my eyes open for suitable locations I thought might work for us.

I reminded them, only half joking, that unless our financial picture improved quickly, additional space would not be necessary. I asked them to think in terms of revenue and space. I also came to the conclusion that expansion—while critical—should be a secondary consideration now, so I mentally pulled it off the table until we had our financial situation resolved. I just couldn't deal with this now.

We then moved on to a report from our fundraising committee, led by my friend Jenny. Fundraising had become a touchy subject lately as our needs grew right before our eyes.

The board members contributed to Second Chance but not very much. None of them were major donors nor did they do much to help me raise funds from those who had the capacity to give. In all fairness, I had not asked for any financial commitment from them when they joined the board. I had left this whole issue up to them and their conscience. [**FACTOR 4, 5, 7**] I really did not want to get into their personal financial situations.

ICK FACTOR 4: POOR COMMUNICATION

ICK FACTOR 5: A CULTURE WITHOUT A SENSE OF RESPONSIBILITY AND ACCOUNTABILITY

ICK FACTOR 7: BOARD MEMBERS WHO DON'T DELIVER

Jenny began, "The fundraising committee has no formal report at this time. We could never get a quorum of people to attend our meetings. We know we need to get working on our gala celebration for next year but I think we have plenty of time to plan a wonderful event." [**FACTOR 5,7**]

ICK FACTOR 5: A CULTURE WITHOUT A SENSE OF RESPONSIBILITY AND ACCOUNTABILITY

ICK FACTOR 7: BOARD MEMBERS WHO DON'T DELIVER

I recognized the opportunity and jumped in. "I have a fundraising item I'd like to discuss. It could really help us out during these tight times. I need a little help over the next few weeks visiting some current and potential donors. I'd like a board member to accompany me in these visits. I believe that with the current crisis it makes more sense to visit people in person, preferably with a member of the board, as a way to really touch hearts and plant a sense of urgency.

I already have several appointments scheduled over the next few weeks with individuals and businesses who have expressed interest in supporting Second Chance, so all I really need is a few of you, for a couple of hours, to join me and lend support in person. These new prospects just want to learn more about us, and how we operate, before they make any commitment. I have been working with most of them for a long time to join us and view them all as viable potential-long term partners and possible major gift donors as well."

The board members looked at each other across the table. [**FACTOR 5, 6, 7**] But just as in the past, no one volunteered to join me to tell our story. They were either too busy or really didn't understand all the giving and estate planning lingo and feared they might hurt our chances rather than help [**FACTOR 5**]. I wasn't really surprised. I'd never been able to get any of them to join me on one of these visits.

ICK FACTOR 5: A CULTURE WITHOUT A SENSE OF RESPONSIBILITY AND ACCOUNTABILITY

ICK FACTOR 6: DISENGAGED BOARD OR INDIVIDUAL DIRECTORS

ICK FACTOR 7: BOARD MEMBERS WHO DON'T DELIVER

I decided again to just do it myself. I could probably do a better job alone than having a reluctant director with me anyway. Disappointed, I dropped the subject.

There was no Old Business to discuss and the remaining committee reports required no immediate board action so we quickly moved to New Business and I opened the floor and invited others to speak. [**FACTOR 8**]

ICK FACTOR 8: INEFFECTIVE MEETINGS

One of our directors, my neighbor from down the street, started things off. "You know I've been thinking about Second Chance lately and I've been wondering if we are doing absolutely everything we can to help the clients find jobs and move forward with their lives.

The number of clients coming to us for help has been growing steadily for the past year or so. Are we really doing all we can to help them? I feel so badly for them and I think we should talk to them and our donors to make sure our programs are comprehensive in the very best way we can make them.

I was reading in a magazine the other day about another nonprofit in Chicago that offers many more programs than we do, and they sounded really interesting. They have programs like job skills training, resume writing assistance, job interview training, computer training, and online job search assistance. These sound like great programs we should consider. How come we don't offer them now?"

There was general agreement around the table that these were great ideas and many of them complemented the services currently offered. Truth be told, they probably made a lot of sense. The board asked me to see if I could investigate this to see what was involved in offering these kinds of programs. They wanted to know what would it take for Second Chance to provide them. They asked me for a report at our next board meeting.

Reluctantly I scratched a quick note on my notepad, adding another item to my list. But I just sat there quietly, my frustration only mounting. [**FACTOR 4**]

ICK FACTOR 4: POOR COMMUNICATION

Soon my sister chirped in. "I think we should consider both a babysitting service and a hot meal program for the clients also, even if it is just breakfast. How can kids concentrate at school on an empty stomach? I bet that Joey kid you told us about probably goes to school hungry, you know Sue?"

I was fuming inside, but remained quiet. [**FACTOR 4**]

ICK FACTOR 4: POOR COMMUNICATION

After a brief general discussion, the board felt I probably had enough on my plate for next month's meeting and agreed to table those last few items for the time being.

With all the new programming suggestions, my head was about to explode. I was amazed at all I was hearing. [**FACTOR 9**]

ICK FACTOR 9: LACK OF A CLEAR STRATEGY

What planet were these people living on? Didn't they hear me when I explained the immediate food crisis we were in? Didn't they understand how many hours I was putting in already, how hard I was working, and the dozens of people I talked to every month about donating money or otherwise supporting Second Chance? Didn't they understand about all the family time I had given up to build and grow Second Chance? Geez... And, where was my husband in all this? Clearly he saw how much time I was putting in, didn't he?

I took a deep breath and tried to remain calm. There was a lot of additional material I had planned to cover during my Executive Director's Report but I decided against it. I didn't know quite how to proceed or what to say, so rather than sounding angry, frustrated, and saying something I might regret, I just asked for a motion to adjourn—made, seconded, done! Sadly, I wasn't surprised.

As the board meeting broke up and everyone began to leave, I heard two directors telling each other how pleased they were with all that Second Chance was doing to help the community and how much they enjoyed serving as directors.

Needless to say, it was a quiet ride back home with my husband. What were they all thinking? It was clear to me the old ways were no longer working. Second Chance was being pushed to the max and we were in real danger of closing our doors. I couldn't stop thinking about Joey and his family. Something just had to be done…

I.F.

ICK FACTORS — CHAPTER 4

Following are the ICK FACTORS specifically mentioned in the chapter. For a complete listing of ICK FACTORS, along with suggestions for how to Break Through these challenges and other helpful resources, please visit section two of the book.

1. NON-STRATEGIC BOARD CANDIDATE SOURCING

4. POOR COMMUNICATION

5. A CULTURE WITHOUT A SENSE OF RESPONSIBILITY AND ACCOUNTABILITY

6. DISENGAGED BOARD OR INDIVIDUAL DIRECTORS

7. BOARD MEMBERS WHO DON'T DELIVER

8. INEFFECTIVE MEETINGS

9. LACK OF A CLEAR STRATEGY

5

THE REALITY CHECK

The next morning I woke up, still frustrated from the board meeting, and feeling very unsettled. I knew I had to figure things out and come up with something. Things had to change and I needed a new perspective. The agency would not survive the way we were operating and I needed much more from the board. I could not fix all of this on my own.

I was amazed at how disengaged the directors were, how uninformed they were about the issues and challenges the agency currently faced, and how hard the staff, volunteers, and I worked to keep things together. [**FACTOR 4, 5, 6, 7**]

ICK FACTOR 4: POOR COMMUNICATION

ICK FACTOR 5: A CULTURE WITHOUT A SENSE OF RESPONSIBILITY AND ACCOUNTABILITY

ICK FACTOR 6: DISENGAGED BOARD OR INDIVIDUAL DIRECTORS

ICK FACTOR 7: BOARD MEMBERS WHO DON'T DELIVER

We'd been making a lot of progress with the clients even under some challenging conditions, yet the board didn't seem to realize just how dire the situation really was. There had been some great progress made every day, but the food and cash shortage crisis threatened everything.

Our board was made up of my friends, neighbors, and my husband for goodness sake! How would I raise these points that were so frustrating to me? [**FACTOR 1, 4**] *I knew I had to be careful, but still, how could they not see what was happening right in front of their eyes? We were doing great work and helping many people but I was being crushed by the weight of it all. Change was needed but I was stumped. This wasn't my area of expertise. Where should I begin, and what exactly should I do?*

ICK FACTOR 1: NON-STRATEGIC BOARD CANDIDATE
SOURCING

ICK FACTOR 4: POOR COMMUNICATION

I climbed in the car, but was overwhelmed by the thought of going right to the office. Instead I went to my favorite coffee shop, *Rivers Edge Cafe*, and ordered my usual—a, mocha. I hoped the smell of freshly ground coffee and hot-from-the-oven pastries would improve my attitude and stimulate my problem-solving abilities.

§

It was a beautiful Fall morning with a slight crisp in the air, but a warm bright sun still shining. After getting my mocha and a pumpkin scone, I sat down outside on the little terrace overlooking the beautiful river. I sat quietly, sipping my drink and gazed out as the water rushed past me. I sat there, and contemplated my current situation with Second Chance.

Whatever problems we had, effort was sure not one of them. I'd never worked harder or put in more time than in these last six months. Same for my staff and volunteers. It had to be something else. I sat there for a while but nothing came to me so I pulled out a notebook, and prepared to put down whatever came to mind.

I wrote down what I thought was working well and not working well. I wanted to capture what I believed were the facts I was facing at Second Chance and any questions I felt needed to be answered. Facts are your friends, right? I forget who said that... But maybe if I started writing down significant facts about Second Chance I would gain some insight.

Clearly what we—what I—was doing, was no longer working to the extent we needed. Our long term prospects looked a little dim. I remained committed to building and growing Second Chance in a way that was healthy and self-sustaining, but I had no idea where to turn.

{If your organization is struggling, but you're not sure why, visit www.IckFactors.com/resourses and take the Break Through Nonprofit Assessment to discover your score.}

I created a document entitled Second Chance: Current Situation and began writing. In a few minutes I had developed an extensive list of all the important facts, givens, or questions

I could think of about the board, the organization, staff and volunteers, and our operations. Twenty minutes later, with my "laundry list" complete, I paused to review.

SECOND CHANCE: Current Situation

• Second Chance has grown in income, clients, and space, steadily over the years from $0 to over $700,000, including in-kind and cash gifts.

• As an organization we still operate the way we did when we first opened our doors. Same process, same paperwork and process flow. [**FACTOR 9**]

• We are facing an unprecedented increase in clients without a comparable increase in cash, food, or personal item donations. When we opened six years ago we served about 100 clients per month and our annual budget was $150,000. Today we are serving 600 per month and our cash and in-kind budget is about $700,000.

• The board is composed of my closest friends who have been with me since day one. They love me and provide great emotional support. They were there to help me open the doors and think through what Second Chance could be. [**FACTOR 1**]

• The board stays out of most of Second Chance's details and relies on me to keep it informed and to provide it with my recommendations for any needed improvements or changes. They never overrule me and always go along with my recommendations. [**FACTOR 1, 6, 7, 10**]

• The board is not sufficiently engaged in what is happening at Second Chance. It just does not "get" the tough situation we are in—the one I am living every day in the food pantry and the closet. [**FACTOR 4, 6, 7, 10**]

• Since none of the directors seem conversant in our issues, maybe I am the problem somehow. [**FACTOR 4**]

• The board usually comes to meetings sort of prepared, sometimes less so, and rarely engages in spirited debate, discussion or disagreement. [**FACTOR 5**]

• No one on the board, including me, has ever run a business of his or her own. We've just figured out how to run Second Chance along the way. [**FACTOR 4, 5, 7**]

• The board has been no help in either fundraising, friend raising, or marketing/advertising. They say they have no experience. [**FACTOR 1, 4, 5, 7**]
None of us are very good at social media stuff. In fact, we barely communicate via email.

• No one on the board qualifies as one of our major donors. Truth be told, the board donates very little in terms of cash or items but does provide volunteer manpower and support at some of our events. [**FACTOR 4, 5, 7**]

• We've never held a retreat or stopped to evaluate where we were or where we thought Second Chance could be in a few years. We just keep working hard every day doing the same thing over and over, only more of it. [**FACTOR 9**]

• We've never discussed what success looked like or how we

should measure it.. We just keep working. We haven't even discussed what progress looks like. [**FACTOR 4, 9**]

• I am not spending enough time thanking our volunteers and donors. We never celebrate when something good happens. I just work them…hard. [**FACTOR 2, 3**]

• All of our volunteers are compassionate, dedicated people who treat our clients with respect. However, they need a lot of constant supervision and guidance, even our experienced ones. This takes up a lot of my time. [**FACTOR 2, 3**]

• Most times, it's quicker for me to just do things, that need to be done rather than asking someone else. [**FACTOR 2**]

• We are small and carry little overhead because we want as much of our donations to go directly to client services. We are a lean organization with very few employees so virtually everything has to come through me, one way or another. Consistently, it is becoming very difficult for me to keep up with everything. Between dealing with all of our day to day employee and volunteer issues, meeting client needs, and our financial obligations. I just don't have time to think…and that's not even to mention working on long-term projects, like our space issues.

• What would happen to Second Chance if I became sick for an extended period of time or were in a serious accident? More importantly, what would happen to our clients?

• If Second Chance is going to become sustainable, increase our ability to serve others, and continue delivering the high-quality service this community has come to expect from us, we must change how we operate.

ICK FACTOR 1: NON-STRATEGIC BOARD CANDIDATE
SOURCING

ICK FACTOR 2: NOT DELEGATING AUTHORITY, TASKS
OR PROJECTS

ICK FACTOR 3: WEAK VOLUNTEER ORIENTATION
AND MANAGEMENT
ICK FACTOR 4: POOR COMMUNICATION

ICK FACTOR 5: A CULTURE WITHOUT A SENSE OF
RESPONSIBILITY AND ACCOUNTABILITY

ICK FACTOR 6: DISENGAGED BOARD OR INDIVIDUAL
DIRECTORS

ICK FACTOR 7: BOARD MEMBERS WHO DON'T
DELIVER

ICK FACTOR 9: LACK OF A CLEAR STRATEGY

ICK FACTOR 10: INEFFECTIVE OR MISSING ANNUAL
PERFORMANCE REVIEWS, FEEDBACK, AND
ASSESSMENTS

I sat back and reviewed what I'd written. After a few minutes, I felt I had a good list to use as a starting point to move forward. Now, what to do with all this? Before tackling that challenge, I moved inside and ordered another coffee.

I was starting to feel a bit better. At least I had begun facing our

51

issues at Second Chance. I no longer felt like a victim of our circumstances, but instead a problem solver.

Knowing the current situation we faced was halfway to determining where we needed to go and how to get there. I had absolutely no idea what to do next but was pretty certain I had accurately summarized where we stood.

I took another sip of my coffee and looked up. A woman across the room had been glancing my way while talking on her phone. She was dressed in business attire with an open laptop and a briefcase at her feet.

She looked familiar but it took me a few minutes to remember who she was. Her name was Kathy. She had been a vice president at the local bank. We had met years ago and participated in a few local community events and fundraisers. When she finished her phone call I smiled and walked over.

"Hi Kathy, it's been a long time. How have you been?" I asked.

"Hi Sue, I'm just great. I retired from the bank last year and now I'm really enjoying doing some part-time consulting, but it still feels like a full-time job some days. How have you been?"

"*Retirement, sounds like heaven*, congratulations! I'm doing well. Lots on my plate these days but the family is healthy and that's important."

"That's for sure! I have to say you look like you just unloaded the weight of the world off of your shoulders," she said.

"I did, or at least half of the weight, for sure" I replied.

"I just stopped in for coffee between appointments. Why is it always the middle appointment that cancels out, never the first or last one of the day? I saw you when I came in a while ago but you seemed deep in thought so I just left you to your thinking."

"I was," I replied. "But it looks like I have part of my problem solved."

"Oh really?"

I told Kathy about Second Chance and the frustrations I had and how I felt better because I had at least identified what I felt were the important issues I needed to address. I shared with her the summary I had just created.

"Nice job, and very interesting." Kathy complimented me. "How do you plan to address all this?"

I smiled. "I haven't exactly figured that out yet."

"I serve on a couple of nonprofit boards in town and would be happy to give you my two-cents worth on this, if you are interested," she continued.

"Absolutely! Thanks."

"I have an appointment in a few minutes around the block. How about you and I meet some time tomorrow?"

"Sounds good!"

Let's meet tomorrow at 10:00 a.m. I have a small office I use and we can go over your list." She handed me her card. "Email me your notes so I can look them over and then let's talk tomorrow."

"Great," I told her. "The list is on its way. See you then."

I.F.

ICK FACTORS — CHAPTER 5

Following are the ICK FACTORS specifically mentioned in the chapter. For a complete listing of ICK FACTORS, along with suggestions for how to Break Through these challenges and other helpful resources, please visit section two of the book.

1. NON-STRATEGIC BOARD CANDIDATE SOURCING

2. NOT DELEGATING AUTHORITY, TASKS OR PROJECTS

3. WEAK VOLUNTEER ORIENTATION AND MANAGEMENT

4. POOR COMMUNICATION

5. A CULTURE WITHOUT A SENSE OF RESPONSIBILITY AND ACCOUNTABILITY

6. DISENGAGED BOARD OR INDIVIDUAL DIRECTORS

7. BOARD MEMBERS WHO DON'T DELIVER

9. LACK OF A CLEAR STRATEGY

10. INEFFECTIVE OR MISSING ANNUAL PERFORMANCE REVIEWS, FEEDBACK, AND ASSESSMENTS

6

THE JOURNEY BEGINS

I arrived at Kathy's office right on time the next day. I even brought us some coffee and a few mini-scones. Walking in, I set the coffee and scones down on the desk. "Hi Kathy! What a convenient office!"

"Thanks Sue! Great to see you again. Thanks for the coffee. I had a chance to look at your list from yesterday. Great summary! Everything was clear, factual, and relevant. There was a lot of information for me to absorb so I spent some time last night thinking about where we might go from here."

"Thanks Kathy. I felt it was important for me to be as objective as possible and to paint as accurate and complete a picture as I could. I didn't want to skim over the high and low points or make any judgments."

"And you did, Sue, great job! The pieces are starting to fall into place for me about Second Chance, but I do have a few questions, specifically about your board, I wanted to discuss. Once I have some of that information we can dive deeper."

"Sure, Kathy." I pulled up a chair in front of her desk. "What would you like to know?"

"Let's start with finding, qualifying, and adding new board members? Do you currently have a process in place for this?"

"Well, when I started Second Chance I asked my husband and a few close friends to join me because they knew of my passion to help others and were very encouraging. I felt I needed people on the board whom I knew well and trusted. They have been with me since the start. We've not added anyone to the board since we started and things seem to have been going well up until recently."

"Sue, did you have any requirements in mind, especially any that were communicated to those individuals when they joined you, so they could be more effective board members?"

"No…" I shrugged. "They were my friends, with the same passion I had, and we all thought a lot alike about how we might help the community. I guess I just figured we'd work things out as we grew."

Kathy nodded. "Did you provide any orientation and training for your directors?"

"No, I tried very hard to keep everyone updated on things as they happened so we all kinda learned and grew and figured things out together."

Kathy scribbled another note on her notepad and continued. "Have any of your directors served on other nonprofit boards?"

"No. We were all new to the nonprofit world, but because we knew so many people in town and had volunteered elsewhere over the years we figured we didn't need a lot of other board experience. Besides, we wanted to do things our own way and not become a replica of others already out there."

I inched back in my chair, feeling put on the spot. I tried to remember that Kathy was trying to help me, but I hadn't been prepared for some of the questions she asked.

Kathy continued. "What big things do you hope to accomplish in the next two or three years? What is your strategy for that?"

"I really haven't had much time to think about the next two to three years. Just thinking about the next two to three months can seem daunting. I guess we'll still be doing what we do now in three years but probably for more people."

"When was the last time you held a board retreat?" Kathy asked.

"We have never actually held an official board retreat. We try to cover everything during our monthly board meetings but we usually run out of time just dealing with the parade of urgent day-to-day issues." I responded.

Kathy smiled reassuringly. "I completely understand. When you have a small organization, it can often be difficult to keep your head above water, especially when you're growing quickly. Sometimes the important planning falls to back burner without anyone really noticing. Your situation is a lot like many other nonprofits.

How does your board help you and Second Chance succeed beside attending all the meetings?"

I thought for a moment. "Well, they have been very supportive and encouraging since the beginning. They volunteer, they donate money at times, and they even helped us paint our offices a few years ago. It is only in the last six months or so that I really could have used their help in a new way. We're just overwhelmed with new clients but the board is unable to help in any significant way."

"Growth can be challenging for any organization. Sounds like your directors might be in a bit over their heads." Kathy paused to take a bite of her scone.

"Sue, what are your board and committee meetings like?"

I paused for a minute before responding. I could see our last board meeting and my friends sitting around the conference table, reassuring me that they trusted my judgment and supported my decisions.

"All the board members are very nice to me and encouraging of what I want to do, but truth be told, the meetings definitely aren't very good," I confessed. "They drag on and on, yet we get very little done. Everyone basically relies on me to update them on our issues, and then they rely on me to come up with the new ideas and solutions to our problems. I guess I don't feel like they are partners with me in this venture, they are just sort of along for the ride."

"I've definitely talked with other nonprofit leaders in your shoes Sue. It's a tough place to be."

I answered Kathy's remaining questions as honestly and frankly as I could. When we finished Kathy jotted down one last note.

"I'm pretty sure I've got it now. I think I have a solid understanding of where things are with Second Chance. Would you like to hear my observations?"

"Absolutely," I said.

"Well, as I see it, there are three critical areas where I think you may need some help. They are *Strategy, Board Development & Governance*, and your approach to Leadership of the organization. Under each of these main areas there are several steps you can take. But to keep it simple for now, let's just discuss the three key areas."

"OK."

"Let me walk you through a few points," Kathy continued.

"Rarely can an organization continue to operate the same way for over six years. Things change over time. The operating environment, clients' needs, personal life situations, the economy, not to mention your staff and your board, they all evolve with time.

Successful nonprofits periodically assess their operating environment, what they are doing, and how successful they are doing it. Being successful when you first started out probably looks very different from being successful today—six years later. That means at different times you have to rethink your tactics to fit the current conditions, if you want to continue being successful and impacting the community. While your mission, vision and values may never change, your goals, objectives, and even structure probably will.

I nodded, feeling a little better. Second Chance really had changed a lot in the past several years. It made sense that we would need to look at things differently if we were going to continue to be successful in the future.

"One thing I noticed was that it looks like you haven't held a Strategic Planning session or board retreat in some time, if at all. Is that right?"

"Yes." I nodded. "We just focus on the next person or family coming through the door and try to serve them as best we can."

"I understand where you're coming from, and those things are very important, Sue, but how do you know whether all the services you are providing to your clients today are what they actually need from you? Maybe their needs have changed from when you first opened your doors. Have you thought about where you are going with all this in the long term? What is your vision for Second Chance three to five years from now?

How do you know that the ways you are spending your money today are the best ways to assure you will be successful, or even still exist, five years from now? How will Second Chance look and what specific services will it provide? What will your clients look like and require in order to succeed, and what will they need most from you?

What should you be doing today so you are ready for whatever challenges or changes you may face down the road? Just working harder and harder only gets you so far... But for now, let's get back to the first of the three areas I wanted to cover with you— *strategy*.

If you want to get on track and build an organization that will sustain itself and be relevant going forward, it seems to me the first issue to address is either developing or refreshing a Strategic Plan. You'll want to adopt a set of Mission, Vision, and Values Statements. From there, you develop a two to three year strategy to get you from here (today) to there (two to three years out). Make sense?"

"It does..." I hesitated. "But we're just a little operation. We don't need some big plan with a bunch of buzzwords and grand intentions. We just want to serve our clients as best we can."

"Sue, every organization needs some kind of written plan in order to know what it's supposed to be doing. Plans help organizations in decision-making, budgeting, staffing, board selection, marketing and everything else. How can you say yes or no to some program, expense or activity if you don't have agreement on what you are trying to accomplish?

In fact I'd say smaller organizations may need a plan even more than larger ones. Smaller nonprofits have very limited resources and therefore a smaller safety net in case something goes wrong, a bad decision is made, or some external event negatively impacts the agency. Smaller agencies have a very small margin for error compared to the big guys so they need to be absolutely certain of whatever decisions they make. One way to do this is with a Strategic Plan. An expensive mistake won't hurt the big guys too badly, but for smaller ones, it could mean shutting the doors."

"I see your point Kathy…So I guess we need a plan."

"Number two in our list of areas to cover is *Board Development & Governance. Board Development* is the term used to describe how an organization identifies, recruits, trains, and utilizes its directors. Governance refers to all significant procedures and the framework under which the board determines to carry out its role. A board will set accountabilities, authorities, working relationships, expectations, etc. There are various governance models and they range from very hands-on to arms length.

Once you have an agreed-upon Vision and Mission, and an understanding of what everyone wants Second Chance to look like in two to three years, you rebuild your board, and organization, around that Vision. While your current board has served you well from when you started out, it may be time to rethink who and what skill sets you currently have. To do this, you have to ask yourself a few questions.

• Is your board performing at its peak ability or can you get more out of it?

• Can your current board, as comprised, get you to that elusive next level?

• Are there skill gaps between what abilities your current board offers and what your future vision will require of the board?

Sue, depending on how you answer these questions, you may need to take a second look at each director and make some tough changes."

"That could be tough." I hesitated. "These are very close friends and neighbors who've been with me since the beginning. How do I remove them from the board? And what about my husband…I can't do that…."

"I get that this situation can be tricky Sue. But there are ways to handle this kind of transition kindly and respectfully. If you want a new energy on your board, and a new active partnership with your board members, you'll probably have to change it up a bit. Your current board may have taken you as far as it can go and to ask more of it may be more than it can deliver.

You have to ask yourself if you are ok with things staying as they are or if you're willing to go through a bit of whitewater rapids to get where your Strategic Plan can take you."

Kathy sensed my anxiety, "Just think of golf for a minute. A golfer starts off on the tee box with a driver, then uses a fairway wood, then goes to a short iron, and finally finishes the hole with a putter. At each stage of progress, a different tool is required. The lifecycle of your nonprofit is no different. It may be time to change some clubs to build and equip Second Chance for the next chapter of its lifecycle."

"Hmm… I guess that makes sense." I replied. "What else should I focus on?"

"The last area we will talk about is your *Leadership* style. You will want to look at how you run or govern the board, its committees and all of your board meetings. My sense is your directors are not being utilized to their full advantage which ultimately hurts your cause.

I find that busy board members are the happiest and the best.

They like to know why they have been recruited onto the board and how they can best serve, so the organization can make a significant impact in the community."

I had never thought of it that way, but it made so much sense.

"So let me see if I understand this. You're saying I need a plan with 3-5 strategies for the next few years that will guide us towards achieving our *Mission*.

Then I use that plan, not only to organize and lead Second Chance, but also to shape the board and fill it with people who are gifted, skilled, or equipped with what we need on the board in order to accomplish that plan. Finally, I have to do a better job leading the board in accomplishing our plan, right?"

"Exactly Sue! I'd only add that all this front-end work will probably have some impact on how Second Chance is organized and how it operates day to day. You may need to get more strategic about the staff and volunteers you recruit. Just like board members, your staff and volunteers should be recruited into your agency based on the skills they have and how those skills fit into the achievement of your approved Strategic Plan."

My head was spinning and I was a bit overwhelmed. But I was really energized as I saw how all this made sense for us. Until now, I just asked for and accepted help from anyone who would join me. All I looked for in volunteers and staff was whether they had a passion for the mission and a willingness to serve. Up until the last year or so, that worked pretty well. But that was about to change.

I had not been very deliberate or selective or forward-thinking about recruiting directors, staff and volunteers, or looking at the specific skills or talents they could provide. I could see now where I'd been missing the boat.

This was going to take some time and effort but I was really jazzed!

"Kathy, you really opened my eyes about a lot of new things today. You must have learned a lot serving on those nonprofit boards. How did you become so knowledgeable about the way successful nonprofits work?"

"As I approached retirement I served on several boards and then went even deeper into nonprofit board leadership once I left the bank. It's been a great experience. I thought I knew a lot about business from my years at the bank, but I've really learned so much more serving on boards."

I saw the opening and jumped right in. "Would you like to serve on my board? We have room for another person."

"Thanks Sue," Kathy replied. "But it's just not a good fit right now. I'm on two boards already as well as another Advisory Council. I just don't have the time to take on another board role and do it the right way."

"Well, how about this," I tried another tack. 'Would you consider giving me some pointers and suggestions for a while as I make the changes needed at Second Chance? I am willing to work on this but I'd feel a lot more confident if I had someone to coach me through the tough spots. We don't have a big consultant budget but I'm sure I can find some money for you, even if I have to pay you myself."

Kathy reflected for a moment, "Tell you what, I'll meet with you periodically over the next few months and we can discuss ways you might improve Second Chance's chances of growing, thriving and sustaining itself. Consider it my gift to the organization. I believe in what you're doing and I'd really like to help you succeed."

"Wow! Thanks Kathy! That would be great! When can we start?"

"How about tomorrow?" Kathy smiled.

"It's a deal!"

7

WHY STRATEGY MATTERS

The next day I arrived at Kathy's office full of anticipation and armed with a lot more questions. I had spent the entire previous evening thinking about everything Kathy had told me and quickly realized I was going to have to make all of this a priority if Second Chance was going to get to the next level.

None of this was going to happen on its own or through sheer luck. I would need to deliberately lead the process and take ownership of it. These changes were not going to happen unless I led them myself and built a convincing case for change.

"Hi Sue, glad you could make it!" Kathy greeted me as I walked into her office.

"Hi Kathy, I just want you to know how grateful I am that you are willing to share your knowledge with me and help me work on Second Chance. I knew we had some challenges but you really helped me understand them better and now you're giving me tools and ideas on how to address them. I really appreciate it."

"Your very welcome Sue, but I must confess I really enjoy

analyzing organizations and developing a plan to make them better. The fact that this one is such an important nonprofit in our community only makes this even better. Shall we dig into the next chapter?"

"Absolutely!" I quickly grabbed a chair and pulled out a notebook and pen.

"Let's start with a direction. Where do you want Second Chance to go and what do you want it to do? We need to develop a vision of what you want to be two to three years from now and then figure out how best for you to get there. We do this with a well defined Strategic Plan."

"Ok, what does a good Strategic Plan look like? How do I build one?" I asked.

"Let me begin by going over a few definitions which I think will help you understand the concept of Strategic Planning and what we are trying to accomplish.

First of all, a *Strategic Plan* is a document that is created by an organization's leaders. It usually involves the board, yet many times includes the agency's top leaders and key staff.

Typically, it can take between one and three days or more to develop the Strategic Plan. It really depends on the size of the organization, the complexity of its mission and structure, and other unique characteristics. But usually, one day is enough for a smaller nonprofit.

I've seen some Strategic Plans as short as one page and as long as eight to ten. Usually, the shorter the plan, the better it is.

A workable Strategic Plan has clarity and focus. Aside from having open and frank discussions as you and your board build the plan, I found the clearer and easier it is to understand, the better chance you have of accomplishing it.

Too many well-written plans, nicely wrapped in leather-bound binders, with fancy lettering and tabs, just end up in a file cabinet because the plans are complicated or difficult to understand and put into action. Fancy words and phrases have no place in the Strategic Plan because the plan has to be read, understood, embraced, and implemented by everyone in the organization. So remember to use clear, simple language that everyone can understand.

{Visit www.IckFactors.com/resourses to download a sample Strategic Planning template to use for your organization.}

The purpose of a Strategic Plan is to describe in broad terms where the organization is headed, its priorities, and what key initiatives need to be accomplished in order to get there. It is usually composed of the following four elements:

1. Vision
2. Mission
3. Values
4. Strategic initiatives
• Goals. (*Specific strategies used to accomplish objectives.*)
• Metrics. (*Numbers used to measure progress.*)

As you can see, Strategic Plans don't describe the specifics of how the mission will be accomplished or list any specific tasks or deadlines. That comes a bit later. I've seen so many Strategic

Plans that are really nothing more than a laundry list of activities to be accomplished rather than high level initiatives to be pursued.

Let's look at a Strategic Plan high level. Then, we'll drill down a bit into each component.

Your Strategic Plan should describe the purpose of the organization, why it exists, and the values you intend to live by as you pursue your mission. In other words, a *Mission Statement* describes the end result of all the anticipated activities of the agency and is silent on the specifics of how it intends to get there."

"What do you mean it is silent on the specifics, and doesn't have any activities listed?", I asked.

"Well, a Strategic Plan doesn't get into the specific operations of an agency or how the plan will be executed. Usually, the "how" part, or the way the agency will operate in order to accomplish its mission is left up to the leaders themselves, not the board. Although the board does have to approve annual budgets, etc." Kathy replied.

"OK, I see. Let's talk about the parts of a plan. What does a *Strategic Plan* look like?"

"Well, the first part of a plan is the *Vision Statement*, which is a high-level statement, or aspiration, describing what your organization would ideally like to see in the future.

For instance, one agency's vision might be to eliminate childhood illiteracy. For another it might be to eliminate homelessness in the community.

"Sue, do you have a Vision Statement for Second Chance?"

"Yes, it is to provide food and clothing to the less fortunate in our community as they work to re-establish their lives following some unanticipated setback".

"I like it Sue, but I think we could make it better."

I didn't really agree with her but I let the comment pass. I had spent a lot of time creating that Vision Statement and was quite proud of it. But Kathy was trying to help, so I thought I'd give her the benefit of the doubt.

"The second part of the plan is a *Mission Statement* which describes why your organization exists and what its role is in achieving your Vision. As an example, I know of a foundation whose Mission Statement is to foster philanthropy and connect donors to the area's needs." Kathy continued.

"Wow. That's very clear and specific." I responded.

"I agree," Kathy offered. "By the way, what is your Mission Statement at Second Chance?"

Sheepishly I had to admit that it pretty much was the same as our Vision Statement, which seemed to confirm Kathy's earlier point that our Vision Statement needed some work.

"Don't worry Sue. I can help you and the board develop a better Mission Statement. But right now, let's move on to the third part—the Values Statement.

A Values Statement describes how your organization will conduct itself as it goes about implementing its plan and pursuing its mission. Think of these as a high level set of ground rules. For some organizations, values are single words or short phrases and for others they may be full sentences. Some common values adopted by organizations include Integrity, Respect, Transparency, Teamwork, and Collaboration.

There are many others to consider. It really depends on what characteristics the board decides are important to the organization. Does Second Chance have a published set of values?"

"No, we just try to respect each other and be appreciative of all the work our board and volunteers do," I said.

"Ok, well we can come back to that, but for now let's move on to the fourth part of a Strategic Plan—Key Strategies. A key strategy, also called a *strategic initiative*, is a high level priority that the organization has decided to pursue. As an example, one key strategy of an agency could be to to expand and bring its services to other parts of the community. This priority would involve evaluating the benefits and implications of either expanding, moving, or opening up a branch service office in another location.

Another strategy may be to evaluate what other programs the agency might offer its client base. One more might be to invest in the profession development and training of key staff and volunteers.

An organization often has three to five of these, but I'd recommend no more than that. Even five may be too many.

If you have too many strategies, you risk spreading the organization too thinly across them all in which case nothing usually gets accomplished. Better to have only two to three and get them right. You can always establish two to three more in the next year or planning cycle.

Sue, do you have any Key Strategies in progress at Second Chance?"

"Well," I responded, "We have lots of issues on our plate and I try to work on them as time permits, like our lack of space and our need for more resources so we can serve all our clients better. We also really need to get active on the internet and with social media, etc..

And I'm not even going to bring up the issue of conducting a current clients' needs analysis. We probably should figure out if what we do today is what clients really need to get back on their feet. And then..."

Kathy interrupted, "See what I mean, Sue? Unless these issues are organized, prioritized and supported by the board, they will just be put in a pile somewhere and forgotten. I don't have to tell you these are extremely important issues—crucial issues—if Second Chance is to really impact the community and be sustainable long term.

I nodded. "No wonder I feel so drained at the end of the day. It's like I really didn't get anything important done. I just kept things moving."

Kathy smiled sympathetically. "I completely understand Sue. We often get caught up in the day-to-day and miss the forest for the trees. But I promise, I can help get you and Second Chance to a better place.

In our earlier discussion I said a Strategic Plan had four parts, but I technically listed six. The last two items on the list—though not officially a part of the Strategic Plan— are intimately related. They are goals and measurements, or metrics.

Your goals are the specific milestones or successes to be achieved along the way of pursuing your strategies. Many people refer to them as SMART goals.

S.M.A.R.T. stands for Specific, Measurable, Achievable, Realistic, and Time bound.

We can talk about these some more later, but for now it's important to recognize that successful organizations always have specific written goals. Each goal has someone assigned to accomplish it within a specific time frame, with a set of metrics to monitor progress. This kind of clarity makes it easier for organizations to achieve their goals in the long run. Without clear goals, a lot of time, money, and effort can be wasted.

I once read where Michael Hyatt, a respected author and consultant, described how all these parts come together. He said something along the lines of:

Values should underpin Vision, which dictates Mission, which determines Strategy, which surfaces Goals... that tell an organization what resources, infrastructure and processes are needed to support a certainty of execution.

You see, everything about your nonprofit cascades, from the Mission, Vision, and Values. They are the foundation documents (along with your bylaws) describing who you are, what you intend to do, and why you are doing it. They are critical to achieving growth and making a bigger impact!"

"I'm starting to see how they could be very helpful."

"Now let's drill down a bit more into why a Strategic Plan is so important to an organization.

A plan serves as a guide for the entire organization. It is a *true north* providing the organization with a direction and a pathway for you to follow to accomplish your mission. A plan keeps everyone's thinking and activity focused in one direction—on your purpose. A good plan will help you:

- Make better decisions more quickly
- Set clearer priorities for everyone involved
- Create a more accurate and realistic budget
- Recruit better board members, staff, and volunteers
- Provide more clarity for the entire team
- Improve focus and communication meetings
- Improve overall effectiveness and efficiency
- Develop and deliver more effective programs

A well-written Strategic Plan gets everyone on the same page and helps focus them on the agency's key issues. A plan also helps agencies avoid:

- Wasted time and money
- Boring and unproductive board and committee meetings
- Indecision and arguments

- Lack of direction
- Repeating the same things, but expecting different results."

"I think having a good plan would really help Second Chance move forward in a better way. But I've tried creating a few high-level plans in the past and somehow they just don't seem to work for us."

"You bring up a great point Sue. There are often gaps between building a Strategic Plan and implementing it. It can be a tough thing to do, but the best plans mean nothing if they are not put into place and executed. Let me give you an example that might help.

Let's say you have held your off-site retreat for Second Chance using a facilitator to lead you through the process. As a part of that, you conducted an internal and external environmental scan of what your current situation is. You now have your gold-plated Strategic Plan with 3-5 key strategies.

The next step is to take those strategies and break them down into smaller bits, which when completed, will result in accomplishing those strategies. This is where those goals we mentioned earlier come in. Those goals are stepping stones to achieving your strategies and your success.

{Visit www.IckFactors.com/resourses *to download a sample Strategic Planning template to use for your organization.}*

Once the goals are established, you need to assign each one to an individual, or a committee, who will be responsible to *drive* it to completion. Include the metrics to measure progress and recognize success once you finally get there. Oh, and remember, all goals need a deadline so be sure to have a date certain for each one.

It's vital that you refer to them periodically to be sure the *owner* is actively working them and progress is being made.

It is always good to start off each of your meetings with a brief report from each of the leader's or owner's goals. That way, nothing falls through the cracks. You don't want to lose sight of the goals as the normal pressures of day-to-day activities interrupt progress on the higher-level initiatives. As the leader, it's your job to ask those tough questions.

Eventually, as significant milestones are reached or goals are accomplished, you should consider some kind of celebration. Nothing energizes the staff and volunteers like recognition, congratulations, and a huge thank you! Don't forget that part…People love it!"

"I'm sure we could definitely benefit from a celebration. I know our staff and volunteers work really hard and sometimes we forget to celebrate what we have accomplished. Sounds like that would be a big boost to morale. Do you have any other guidance for helping the team execute the plan?"

"John Kotter, one of my favorite business authors and thinkers, identified 8 steps to a successful plan implementation in his book *Leading Change*. In summary, they are:

• Create Urgency: Explain to everyone why things have to change and what may happen if nothing is done.

• Build a powerful coalition: Convince people of the need for change and build coalitions of teams committed to seeing it through.

• Create a vision for change: Provide a picture of what the change will look like as it happens so people can understand it. Otherwise, they will make things up on their own.

• Communicate the vision: To everyone, all the time, repeatedly.

• Remove obstacles: Eliminate things that get in the way of your chosen path. They will undermine you and your efforts.

• Create short-term wins: Find meaningful things to celebrate along the way. People get motivated by successes as they go through the tough changes being implemented.

• Build on the change: Start using as much of the new system as possible, as soon as you can. Show everyone that it is here to stay so they may as well get on the bandwagon.

• Anchor the changes in your culture: Make the new methodology a part of the fiber and foundation of your nonprofit. Don't let people backslide into the old ways.

Some of these concepts might be helpful for Second Chance.

The last thing I want to mention on Strategic Planning is how organizations use their Strategic Plan for positive impact and great results. I touched on this earlier but let's revisit it for a moment.

You might have the very best plan ever written, but if it just sits on the shelf in a nice, leather bound book, it will do you absolutely no good. So, let me suggest some tactics, or pointers, that will help you implement your plan effectively.

Ways to use your Strategic Plan:

• As a communication tool to create a clear purpose for the organization, help everyone understand the importance of their role, and to provide clarity to constituents, donors, key strategic partners, and others.

• To provide focus and direction to management and staff. This helps gain commitment, clarity, and buy-in from the staff, volunteers, and board.

• To build your budget, making the process clear and focused.

•For easier and more consistent decision-making.

• To ensure operational excellence Strategic Plans help leadership organize the agency for maximum impact.

• To stay focused, avoiding short-term, passive–reactive thinking.

• As a road map for execution, which is critical to achieving an organization's mission.

• As a model for deeper, internal planning. Sometimes, organizations will develop mini Strategic Plans to complement and further their overall strategies. These mini strategies work to support the high level strategies approved by the board. For instance, a strategy to increase the level of donations, or a strategy to implement a marketing or social media plan to improve outreach, and increase awareness.

• To promote organizational alignment. The best way to describe alignment is to show you this picture."

With that, Kathy drew the following chart on a sheet of paper and slid it over to me.

GOAL ALIGNED MODEL

"Thanks Kathy! This chart really brought it all together for me. Now I see how all the pieces we've been discussing fit together and support each other."

"Sue, this chart shows you how everything works together, in what I call 'alignment'. It shows how each piece of your organization is interrelated, much like a puzzle. Each area complements and works together in support of your mission. Tight alignment insures you are wisely and most efficiently using your people, your resources, and your systems, in achieving your mission.

Everything cascades from your mission, vision, and values. Once you've developed a compelling vision of the future, and clarified what your mission is, in pursuit of that vision, and identified the values under which you will operate, everything else needs to fall into place or cascade from the previous step.

Your key strategies and goals are based upon your mission, vision, and values. From those flow the culture you wish to create which determines your staffing, training, and hiring practices.

Any partnerships or strategic relationships you develop would be based on all the above. This would include the composition of your board, your bylaws, your processes, procedures and rules of governance. Finally how you market yourself (your branding and positioning) should also flow from this.

All of this alignment is the result of a well-thought out strategy. Pretty neat, huh?"

"This is great. I can't wait to try it!"

"Well," said Kathy, "This is where we stop for now. Once you conduct your retreat and develop your Strategic Plan, we can meet and discuss how to get the most out of your board."

8

THE PLAN FOR ACTION

After my last meeting with Kathy, I called a meeting with the board members to discuss having a retreat to address the issues that had been bothering me. I went into some detail on why I felt we needed to get together for an extended meeting and why I felt an outsider should lead the session. In their minds, the board felt we were ok as is, but they trusted my judgement and went along with my recommendation.

I was so grateful they approved my request and authorized the expense involved, contingent on their approval of the facilitator. I felt that was a reasonable request so I agreed to search for someone I felt would be good match for us.

I asked Kathy for her recommendations, and she gave me the names of three facilitators. After speaking with all three, I felt the most comfortable with the second one I had spoken with—Frank. He had a relaxed style and struck me as a good listener.

When I spoke with Frank he asked a lot of questions about Second Chance and the board and didn't try to force any prepackaged solutions on us. He seemed to be trying to figure out how he might best serve us. I sensed he was going to work with our best interests in mind, which was reassuring. The following week I scheduled a meeting with him.

I learned Frank had once been a part-time Executive Director at a very small nonprofit while working full-time in the business world. He had also served on a couple nonprofit boards as well. Two years ago, he left the business world and went full-time into nonprofit work.

After just a few minutes, I could tell Frank knew the agency world and understood where I was coming from and what we needed—*what I needed*—to get Second Chance on the right track.

"Sue," he said, "The issues you face are very common in the nonprofit world. In fact most of my clients come to me needing help with their Strategic Plan. They're afraid that the plan will make them bureaucratic or lock them into a direction that isn't as effective and that they can't change.

With everything you're telling me I think you're wise to update your Strategic Plan and get everyone's agreement. It's really the best place to start when you have several issues to resolve.

Some organizations are afraid to go off into a retreat because they feel they'll be opening up a can of worms, with the meeting ending with disagreement and even hurt feelings. I want you to know that I have facilitated many Strategic Planning sessions, with large and small agencies, start ups and well established agencies, too. If the session is properly facilitated and everyone comes with the right frame of mind and motivation, the retreat can be an invigorating, exciting event.

I really like the purpose of Second Chance and the passion you bring. I would enjoy helping you chart out a course for the next two or three years and help create strong alignment of all your resources to achieve your goals."

"Thanks Frank! How would you recommend we proceed if we did this?" I asked.

"Because this would be the first significant board retreat ever held by Second Chance, I think the best outcome would be to develop a full Strategic Plan document containing a mission, vision, values statement, and a set of key priorities.

Since we only have one day, Sue, you and your team would need to drill down into more detail and develop your own specific goals for each key priority at a follow-up meeting, but I am happy to take a look at them once you've finished them."

Frank assured me that creating a good set of foundational documents like these, would serve alongside our by-laws and provide a solid footing on which to build our future plans. He shared that this would help us grow a sustainable Second Chance and increase the impact in the community. I was stoked!

§

In our preliminary discussions, Frank suggested I consider including our employees and any key volunteers in the retreat. He felt they could shed valuable new light on a variety of operational details our board probably knew nothing about. I agreed.

"I think a clear direction for the next few years, and a way to be sure we are using our resources wisely and most effectively, is exactly what we need. What are the first steps we need to take to get this ball rolling?"

"Sue, I think it would be wise for me to meet with all, or at least part of your board, once the idea of a retreat has been approved. We want them to realize that I'm there to facilitate on behalf of Second Chance to get it the best possible outcome. I am not coming with any agenda and it's important for them to know that and have confidence and trust in me to do the best job for all of you."

§

Frank gave me some dates and times he was available and I made arrangements for him to meet with the board so each director could get to know him and hopefully gain confidence in him and the process. I encouraged the directors to prepare any questions they might have for him, and to ask Frank anything they wanted to know.

As it turned out, the meeting went very well. The board saw Frank had no hidden agenda and would give everyone a chance to air their thoughts. He connected with all of the directors almost immediately.

§

I called Frank the next day to firm up our arrangements. He had a lot of suggestions for me. In order to prepare for the retreat Frank suggested the board do some homework in advance. He had a lot of great ideas on how to help us get ready. He asked that we create a packet of materials for each director including:

1. The latest financials

2. Any data showing results from our programs

3. Cost information related to services provided

4. Donor profile information, in aggregate, by donation ranges

5. Any trending information over the last three years about the clients, such as:

- The numbers served
- The number of new versus repeat clients
- How long clients used the services of Second Chance

6. And any other measurements I felt were relevant

Frank and I went over all the logistical details about the event itself including the facilitation ground rules he intended to use.

I agreed to find a conference room or some facility that could accommodate our needs. I knew just the room—a conference room at the bank where we did our banking. When I called I found they were most gracious and happy to host us.

I was very excited and couldn't wait for the retreat. I would be ready, the board and staff would be ready, and I was committed to creating a solid plan to cover the next two to three years.

§

A few weeks later Frank led our all-day board retreat. It was a long but productive day. What an experience! We had a lot of great ideas flying all over the room and everyone really got into it. Thank goodness we had Frank there.

He brought balance, kept us on point and kept us moving forward, bringing order when we needed it. He also captured and consolidated all the ideas we formulated so we could concentrate on brainstorming and not note-taking. By the end of the day, we had a working version of our plan.

Second Chance: Strategic Plan Retreat Results

Vision: A Community Bringing Hope and Assistance to the Less Fortunate

Mission: Food, Clothing, and Support for People in Need

Values: Community, Compassion, Hope, Dignity, Service

Key Strategies:

1. Determine Second Chance's best option to expand its service area, including moving to a larger facility, opening additional locations, or expanding in its current location.

2. Determine what program offerings are needed and would best serve the clients Second Chance assists today.

3. Develop a marketing and community outreach strategy to build name recognition and create greater awareness of

Second Chance and its operations in the community.

4. Develop a mid- and long-range fundraising strategy to ensure Second Chance has the financial and in-kind support necessary to continue meeting the growing number of clients seeking help.

As we wrapped up the day, Frank offered a few ideas on next steps, pending formal board approval of the new plan.

STRATEGIC PLAN IMPLEMENTATION TIPS

1. Communicate the plan to everyone as soon as possible including major donors, key partners, and any other significant supporters and friends of the agency.

2. Create a sense of urgency within the agency explaining why we can no longer continue operating as we had.

3. Create a logical plan for implementing changes. What tasks need to be accomplished and in what order.

4. Create a feedback loop within the Second Chance community to hear how the plan and its changes are being received and understood.

5. Prepare for some resistance. Listen carefully to everyone's concerns. Develop and deliver powerful talking points explaining why Second Chance could no longer stay where it was, and how the benefits of moving on to this new level far outweighed continuing to do business as usual.

6. Frequently remind every one of the plan's benefits.

7. Create a number of "quick wins" so volunteers, staff, the board, and others can see benefits of the new plan as soon as possible.

8. Prepare yourself to wrestle with the following issues:

• What organizational and structural changes may be needed?

• How will the budget change?

• What should Second Chance stop doing immediately, begin doing immediately, or do more frequently starting now?

• What elements or characteristics of Second Chance must be protected and encouraged at all costs?

• How will this new plan impact future hiring and recruiting, and board member selection?

After we finished, I asked Frank if he had seen Strategic Plans fail. And if yes, why? I wanted to know what I should be focusing on assure ours would be a success.

He explained what he called a basic fact of life in the planning community. Most Strategic Plans fail. Sometimes the plans are weak and unworkable so they fail.

Of the solid plans that are workable, 90% of businesses fail to execute the strategy because of leadership's failure to communicate the plan, not being certain everyone understands the plan, or because no one takes individual ownership over the plan's implementation.

Frank told me the biggest reasons for failure are poor communication, poor follow-through by leadership, and not using an outside facilitator who brings balance and objectivity.

He stressed that it was critical that I set the stage early in the process for everyone by creating a sense of urgency, using clear, simple language — no buzz words and no jargon. I had to set the stage for change by explaining that maintaining the status quo was no longer an option.

He also gave me several other reasons plans fail. These included:

• Not linking daily activities and decisions to the plan. *People needed to see that everything being done and decided is based on the plan and that the plan is alive and well and being followed daily*

• Not reminding everyone frequently why the changes are being made

• Not "owning" the responsibility for implementation of the plan myself

• Not celebrating successes as they occur
Not staying in close communication with the board and its chair to be sure they are actively supporting each other and reinforcing the plan

• Not making the tough calls for which the new plan calls.

• Letting implementation of the plan get bogged down or

ignored due to the normal pressures and distractions of day-to-day operations at Second Chance

I remembered several of these key points from my discussions with Kathy. It reaffirmed my faith in what Frank was telling me.

§

At our next board meeting the new Strategic Plan was approved in short order. For the first time in a long time I felt we all were on the same page. I only hoped it would last.

I distributed copies of the plan to all directors, staff, and key donors. I was so excited! I rolled out the plan to everyone and we began using it right away.

With our new Strategic Plan in place, I could finally see how things were supposed to work together. In the past, everything was just an activity or a requirement or a task. Now with our plan in place, nearly everything we did seemed to have a home, and a purpose, and make more sense.

We began to question anything that did not seem to fit our strategy and made a conscious effort to either stop doing it or recommitted to it as being an important part of our program.

9

THE KEYS TO A GREAT BOARD

A few weeks later Kathy and I met again at her office to discuss the second area of improvement–Building the Board. I walked into her office with the now-typical coffee and snacks and settled into the chair opposite Kathy.

"Hi Sue! Are you ready for our next adventure— *building a better board?*"

"You bet!" I responded.

"Building an effective board is a year-round job. Successful nonprofit leaders are always looking for board member candidates, whether they have any current openings or not. They maintain an active candidate list and keep it handy. It's always better to have too many candidates available rather than too few.

One of the biggest mistakes nonprofit leaders make is to go out looking for new directors at the last minute to fill an opening, just as one or more directors are leaving the board, as a result of an expired term.

Since everything starts at the top, a high-quality board is a must, and you just can't put one together at the last minute. It takes time to identify, qualify, recruit and then train the candidate so he or she can become an active, engaged director as soon as they are elected to office."

"What should I be looking for in a potential candidate?" I asked.

"There are a couple of layers to answering that question but let me first say you should never be in a rush to find someone just to fill an open board spot. The ultimate goal is to get the right people on the board, doing the right thing.

Best-selling author Jim Collins once said,

Start by getting the right people on the bus, the wrong people off the bus, and the right people in the right seats.

His research validated that every successful organization has a solid board and leadership team. If there are significant problems in an organization, like a nonprofit agency, then there is likely a problem with the board as well," Kathy continued.

It is important to have the right mix of people and skill sets on the board, based on where the nonprofit is in its lifecycle, and where it intends to go. Personally, I like board members who, in addition to specific professional skill sets, also have the gifts of wisdom, experience, and critical thinking.

It's also important that you don't assume good volunteers, good neighbors, or major donors automatically make good directors. They usually don't. The skill set required to be a good board member is unique.

Look for board candidates who can help you achieve the agency's mission. For instance, your Strategic Plan tells you where the organization is headed and therefore the kind of skills that may be helpful to have on the board. Try to find individuals who can support the direction Second Chance is headed through their skills, experience, connections, etc.

I also suggest you look at people who have demonstrated a commitment to your calling and your mission, and have good judgment or critical thinking skills which can be transferred onto the board and utilized. Hopefully, you can find these people as part of your core volunteer group or key partners. I think you should strongly consider those who have been actively engaged with Second Chance, perhaps serving on some committee at first, so you have a sense of how they work with others in the nonprofit environment.

{Visit <u>www.IckFactors.com/resourses</u> to download a sample Board Profile Worksheet to use for your organization.}

"Thanks Kathy, that makes a lot of sense. What else should I be looking for?"

"You'll want to find candidates who will recognize and carry out the legal responsibilities and duties of a board member. For instance, officially a director has three legal duties:

• *Duty of Care*—requiring each board member to exercise what the general public would recognize as a "reasonable" level of care in carrying out his or her duties. In other words, there is no obligation a board member be perfect, but he/she must act in a way such that ordinary people would expect one to act, assuming similar circumstances.

• *Duty of Loyalty*—requiring each board member to give undivided allegiance—no conflicts of interest—when making decisions about the organization. They can never obtain personal gain from actions as a board member, and must always act in the best interest of the organization.

• *Duty of Obedience*—requiring a director to remain faithful to the organization's mission and take no action that is inconsistent with the central goals of the organization.

Underlying these duties is a board member's fiduciary responsibility to serve in an ethical position of trust, especially in the protection and use of the organization's resources.

In addition to recruiting candidates who can fulfill these duties you'll also want to look for candidates who will embrace and uphold the mission, vision, values, and strategy of Second Chance.

You'll want candidates who will recognize the critical role they play in protecting the agency's assets and providing appropriate financial oversight. There may be some other qualifications you want to include but I'd say these are the most important.

After you've identified and started recruiting your ideal candidates you'll want to spend some time with each one reviewing subjects they should understand before going any further. These would include:

• Reviewing the director job description, duties and

responsibilities

• Any specific expectations or plans you may have for this candidate once they are on the board. This transparency helps set clear expectations on both sides

• An overview of some of the important issues the board currently faces

• The mission, vision, and value statements

• History of the organization

• The Board Policy Manual

• Code of Conduct Policy

• Conflict of Interest Policy

• And anything else you feel is best discussed up front before the candidate or the board decides to take that final step

{Visit www.IckFactors.com/resourses to download tips for successful Board Orientation and Training.}

Once you have your board in place it's important it is led effectively by the Board Chair, even though you, as Executive Director, still play a significant role with the board."

I jumped in quickly, "Actually, Kathy, I'm on the board and I am also its Chair. Is that a problem?"

"It's understandable that as the founder you would be on the board and likely serving as chairperson, but at some point soon, I recommend you relinquish the chairperson's role and either step off the board or have a non-voting seat."

From a conflict of interest standpoint, that makes the most sense for Second Chance, although I understand that may be a bigger jump than you are willing to take just now."

"But Second Chance was my idea and was created from a lot of my blood, sweat, and tears. Why should I step down?" I cringed.

"Well, you have to remember the board has a fiduciary duty to protect the organization. Since you're also sitting as a director you are in effect supervising and leading yourself in your capacity as Board Chair. This is a significant conflict of interest and can cause problems, if not outright trouble down the road.

It is becoming more and more common in the nonprofit world for diffrent people to serve as Executive Director and Board Chair. Those duties should be split between two people. You may want to give this careful consideration."

§

"For now, let's move on to another topic—how *effective boards operate*. If you're going to recruit an A-Team of high-value directors, one which has the kind of reputation that attracts outstanding board candidates, you need to run the board and its meetings effectively. High-value directors and candidates will not waste their time at ineffective meetings or on boards that accomplish little.

High-quality candidates are there to make a difference. Unless they feel they are contributing to the overall good, they'll leave. Here are some suggestions on how to effectively lead nonprofit boards:

1. Adopt a practical set of governance principles. This means you need to establish clarity between the roles of the board, you as the Executive Director, and the staff. Everyone has a role, no gaps and no overlap. Then decide how the board will operate in carrying out its duties.

2. Determine what kind of board Second Chance needs.

• At one extreme are working boards, which in addition to their fiduciary and oversight duties, get involved in some day-to-day activities and lots of detail. These are roll up the sleeves boards, and are typical of start ups and very small nonprofits. They are said to be very involved with both the "ends" (purpose of the agency) and the "means" (how it will get there).

• At the other extreme are boards that have virtually no involvement in the details but focus solely on their oversight role and fiduciary responsibilities. They establish the boundaries an Executive Director can work within and they leave implementation up to him or her. They focus on the "Ends".

• In truth, many boards operate somewhere in the middle, but that can be dangerous.

3. Run well-paced and crisp board and committee meetings. The agendas should avoid a lot of details the board really has no need to know, and instead address high-level issues, especially

during the full board meetings. Your committee meetings may get a little more detailed, but guard against turning your board or board committees into extensions of your staff. That is not their job.

4. Maintain transparency and clarity in all communications between you and the board.

5. Install term limits. The kind of limitations isn't as important, just be sure to have something!

6. Use board committees fully. This is where the heavy lifting and detailed work gets done. It is up to committees to research and vet major issues and then report back to the board for recommendations, discussions and appropriate action.

7. Use a standard meeting agenda template, including a consent agenda, to keep meetings moving along at a good pace.

8. Actively manage board discussions at meetings, keeping everyone on topic and do not allow them to drag on, or veer off into other areas.

9. Hold people accountable for their commitments. You have to hold people to their word or you will have chaos.

10. Create and maintain a Board Policy Manual with your bylaws, Strategic Plan, and any policy decisions the board makes, like a Risk Management Policy, Emergency Succession Plan, Expense Reimbursement Policy, Compensation Policy, Conflict of Interest Policy, a Gift Acceptance Policy etc. That way you always have the most up-to-date collection of board policies at your fingertips, together in one reference book.

There is a lot more we could talk about regarding building and leading a board but if you can adopt and implement most of the items we discussed today, you'll be well on your way to becoming a Best in Class, outstanding nonprofit agency."

"Thanks Kathy, I really appreciate your insight and experience, but how do I go about doing all this? There's so much to do and it's hard to know what comes first."

"Sue, I think the sense of overwhelm you are feeling is very understandable. You'd like to rebuild the board as soon as possible yet at the same time you want to install a lot of new ideas and make changes that your current directors may resist.

The truth is, you will probably have to work on both a new board and your new ideas at the same time. It's going to take longer than you'd like, so patience will be very important. Just keep your eye on the prize as you make steady progress, knowing you are getting closer to your desired future with each step.

One way to kickstart change is to create a Governance Committee. This committee has several responsibilities and one important one is to identify, qualify, and recruit all new board candidates. Then once the new candidates are on board, the Governance Committee provides proper orientation and training for the newly elected directors, as well as all current directors.

Normally, it's the entire board's responsibility, as well as yours, to find board candidates that fit your board's needs. New candidates should be put through a qualification process and have a chance to work with board members and staff on a project or two, to see how well they fit into the agency, the board, and the culture. If things look good, they should be invited for an interview so both sides can explore how well it might work and clarify mutual expectations.

Since you don't currently have a Governance Committee I suggest you ask the board to establish one and appoint two to three current directors along with yourself to serve on it. Then, with a full understanding of the implications of your Strategic Plan, encourage each board member to mentally go through his or her existing network to see whether anyone might fit the current and future needs of Second Chance. Open this funnel as wide as possible to be sure you don't miss any high-quality candidates.

Before too long your Governance Committee will have a good list of candidates to evaluate. From that list find the top two or three, and seek the approval of the Governance Committee to pursue them.

I was getting a little overwhelmed. "I guess this is going to take some time…"

"Yes, it will take a little while Sue, but this is not something you want to rush through. You are better off leaving a board seat unfilled until the right candidate comes along, than just filling it with anyone, no matter how nice they are, how good a friend they are, or how much they've donated in the past.

Remember, this is a never-ending process. You and the current directors should maintain that confidential list of viable candidates we discussed earlier so you can keep an eye on them and how they relate to Second Chance even before they are formally invited to apply.

Keep in mind, some high-value board candidates will already be serving on a board and will not be available when you are ready for them. Review your list periodically and be sure to keep in touch with those you hope to recruit later."

Kathy stood and walked around to the front of her desk, taking the chair next to mine. She smiled. "Sue, try not to get overwhelmed by all this. Turning over and replenishing a board will take time, even if you are lucky enough to get all the new candidate selections right.

In the meantime, there is a lot you can do right now to raise the bar for board service at Second Chance. You can start by redefining the expectations of board service almost immediately. Next week, let's talk about how best-in-class boards operate and your role in making that happen."

I thanked Kathy for all her help and told her I'd think about what kind of board would be best for us over the next two to three years. I also agreed to start building a list of potential candidates who would fit that bill.

As I walked to my car I was a little concerned how my current directors would feel about changing up the board, but I did have a couple of open seats available so I could start there.

Technically, no one would have to be removed at this point for me to add some new life.

I hope that as a few of my current directors saw how their positions were being impacted by these changes they might just opt out on their own. Our Strategic Planning session and the document we developed were turning points for Second Chance and I hoped they would see it as a logical juncture to decide if they wanted to "sign up" for the new ways that were ahead.

10

LEADING THE BOARD

I had come to feel right at home in Kathy's office by now, so when I arrived for my appointment the next week, I spread out my material on the desk and jumped right in. I was excited! I think we both saw progress being made and wanted to keep moving forward. "What's on the agenda for today Kathy?"

Kathy started. "Hi Sue! Today we revisit the topic of Board Development, starting with a good strategy for meetings. All successful nonprofits have several things in common. One of those things is that they hold effective meetings. Let's talk about how to make your board and committee meetings better.

"Sounds good! Our meetings definitely aren't the best. They can be long, boring, poorly attended, and often uninspiring, but I don't know how to change them. I just know we don't get much accomplished." [**FACTOR 5, 8, 10**]

ICK FACTOR 5: A CULTURE WITHOUT A SENSE OF
RESPONSIBILITY AND ACCOUNTABILITY

ICK FACTOR 8: INEFFECTIVE MEETINGS

ICK FACTOR 10: INEFFECTIVE OR MISSING ANNUAL PERFORMANCE REVIEWS, FEEDBACK, AND ASSESSMENTS

"I'll get into all of that, don't worry," Kathy nodded. "But let's start with your committees and how you use them.

Nonprofits are shifting away from the traditional model of authorizing a lot of standing Board Committees. Boards have finally discovered the concept of "delegation" and learned that using ad hoc committees—sometimes called Task Forces, are usually much more effective.

These committees are created to address a specific issue, like expansion, or a special HR issue like a compensation study, etc. They can be a great way to get your best thinkers to focus on one specific issue. You can even bring in non board members to serve on a specific committee as well. Once the ad hoc committee completes its work, it is disbanded. [**FACTOR 5, 6, 7**]

ICK FACTOR 5: A CULTURE WITHOUT A SENSE OF RESPONSIBILITY AND ACCOUNTABILITY

ICK FACTOR 6: DISENGAGED BOARD OR INDIVIDUAL DIRECTORS

ICK FACTOR 7: BOARD MEMBERS WHO DON'T DELIVER

Having fewer standing committees, and instead using ad hoc committees, tends to reduce the bureaucracy of the board. If you have six or seven standing committees, they can bog down a board meeting because each one usually wants to make a report at every meeting, sometimes with little to say. Also, it can be hard to disband a standing committee, so if you give it a specific task and let them know the committee will be over once its work is done, it is much easier to shut it down later. I have even found you may get some outside top talent to join the committee work if you assure them the committee has an end date. [**FACTOR 4, 5, 6, 7, 8**]

ICK FACTOR 4: POOR COMMUNICATION

ICK FACTOR 5: A CULTURE WITHOUT A SENSE OF RESPONSIBILITY AND ACCOUNTABILITY

ICK FACTOR 6: DISENGAGED BOARD OR INDIVIDUAL DIRECTORS

ICK FACTOR 7: BOARD MEMBERS WHO DON'T DELIVER

ICK FACTOR 8: INEFFECTIVE MEETINGS

Successful boards typically refer important topics to a committee for investigation, research, and further review. [**FACTOR 2, 4, 5, 6, 7, 8**] There is nothing worse than an entire board getting bogged down in discussion because of a lack of facts, or getting lost in the fine details.

A board committee can be worth its weight in gold, because it will conduct the necessary research off-line, on its own time, and then present findings and a recommendation at the board meeting. This is much more professional and efficient, and a great way to respect your board members' time.

ICK FACTOR 2: NOT DELEGATING AUTHORITY, TASKS OR PROJECTS

ICK FACTOR 4: POOR COMMUNICATION

ICK FACTOR 5: A CULTURE WITHOUT A SENSE OF RESPONSIBILITY AND ACCOUNTABILITY

ICK FACTOR 6: DISENGAGED BOARD OR INDIVIDUAL DIRECTORS

ICK FACTOR 7: BOARD MEMBERS WHO DON'T DELIVER

ICK FACTOR 8: INEFFECTIVE MEETINGS

Using this practice often will keep board meetings moving and productive. If additional research and discussion is required before board action can be taken, the matter is referred back to the committee for additional work. If the issue is ready for vote, the board votes and acts accordingly.

It's also helpful to set board and committee meeting dates in advance and to clarify attendance expectations. Some recommend posting a twelve month calendar with all board and committee meeting dates. I'd also post any key dates for the board to block off in their calendars, like galas, fundraising events, etc.

I suggest you send out the agenda and all supporting material at least a week before the scheduled meeting with a reminder that the meeting will be conducted in such a way that assumes everyone has familiarized themselves with the material."

"That may be tough, since I haven't insisted they do this in the past."

"Sure, it may be a challenge at first, but the alternative is to continue experiencing the type of meetings you are having now. How would that feel?"

"Point well-taken." I agreed.

"Another tip to avoid getting bogged down in meetings is to keep the agendas high-level [**FACTOR 8**]. The board doesn't need to know every little detail about day-to-day operations but it must be kept informed of all key issues the agency faces and progress on the Strategic Plan. One suggestion is to create your own customized board reporting template, or Dashboard Report Template to provide a quick and effective visual progress update. You just prepare a list of all your top priority issues and then assign a grade to each one. Some boards use a red light, yellow light, green light approach. Others use a numbering system, some use a thumbs up, thumbs down, thumbs level indicator.

ICK FACTOR 8: INEFFECTIVE MEETINGS

Just by looking at the report, the board can quickly see the status of every key initiative and then hone in on those with troubling grades. This saves a lot time and keeps the board's focus where it should be. The board quickly sees where progress has been made and where problems may be lurking, and in need of its attention.

Certainly, if they want to dive deeply into some topic that is their prerogative and they have every right to do so. But most of the time, they will be satisfied with just an overview.

It's really important to actively manage the meetings and discussions. This helps keep everyone on topic, avoids repetition and meandering off point, and keeps any one individual from monopolizing the conversation. It may seem hard at first, but after the first time or two, people will come to understand that your purpose is to keep things moving to protect everyone's time. In fact they will come to respect and appreciate your efforts.

The one mistake many boards make is to have a fruitful and productive conversation on some important topic and then fail to record what next steps are required, who is responsible to take them, and by what date [**FACTOR 5, 8**]. If you don't capture and publish this information, it's very difficult to continue making progress between the board and committee meetings. You want to keep the momentum moving between meetings and the best way to do that to be sure everyone understands what they commit to do next and by when.

ICK FACTOR 5: A CULTURE WITHOUT A SENSE OF RESPONSIBILITY AND ACCOUNTABILITY

ICK FACTOR 8: INEFFECTIVE MEETINGS

You can also help to keep things moving between board or committee meetings by reaching out to your Board Chair and some directors each month. This will help you build a strong relationship with each individual board member. A quick phone call, just to check in with them, goes a long way. They will feel included, important, and plugged in to what's going on, as well as more vital to the success of the agency. Sometimes, you might not even discuss agency issues but instead keep the phone call entirely personal and general. I think you'll find they would respond very well to this. [**FACTOR 4**]

ICK FACTOR 4: POOR COMMUNICATION

If you really want to put your board on the fast track for improvement then I suggest, your Governance Committee ask everyone how they felt about the meeting and what could've been done to improve it, at the conclusion of each meeting. That feedback is invaluable. In short order, your board and committee meetings will become significantly more effective.

One last thing about meetings. It's always better when the Board Chair and the Executive Director discuss and agree on the agenda and handouts in advance. In your case I would be sure to sit down with your Executive Committee —the group of individuals within the board who have the authority to make decisions and ensure that those decisions are carried out — and do this together. You will have much better meetings, with more accomplished. Because everyone had a hand in crafting the meeting they will feel like they have a better overall understanding. [**FACTOR 4, 6, 7, 8, 10**]

ICK FACTOR 4: POOR COMMUNICATION

ICK FACTOR 6: DISENGAGED BOARD OR INDIVIDUAL DIRECTORS

ICK FACTOR 7: BOARD MEMBERS WHO DON'T DELIVER

ICK FACTOR 8: INEFFECTIVE MEETINGS

ICK FACTOR 10: INEFFECTIVE OR MISSING ANNUAL PERFORMANCE REVIEWS, FEEDBACK, AND ASSESSMENTS

I also suggest you begin creating a Board Policy Manual as soon as possible [**FACTOR 4**]. This will take some time but is well worth it. A Board Policy Manual contains all significant board decisions on policy, protocols, procedures, etc.

ICK FACTOR 4: POOR COMMUNICATION

This document can provide a great way to collect, monitor, and enforce all ongoing procedures, protocols, and policies the board has adopted. It should contain all the basic foundational documents of your organization like:

- Bylaws
- Job descriptions
- Latest financial reports
- 501(c)(3) approval
- All existing policies and procedures, and their updates.

{Visit www.IckFactors.com/resourses *to download guidelines for creating an effective Board Policy Manual.}*

Finally, successful boards are really good at providing orientation and training for new board members, as well as periodic refreshers for existing directors. Simply assuming new directors understand what's expected of them and how to conduct themselves can be a recipe for disaster.

You can risk losing great new directors because they don't know enough about the agency, or the job they were recruited to do. [**FACTOR 6, 7, 10**]

ICK FACTOR 6: DISENGAGED BOARD OR INDIVIDUAL DIRECTORS

ICK FACTOR 7: BOARD MEMBERS WHO DON'T DELIVER

ICK FACTOR 10: INEFFECTIVE OR MISSING ANNUAL PERFORMANCE REVIEWS, FEEDBACK, AND ASSESSMENTS

Taking time periodically to review the organization's Mission, Vision, and Values, and its key operational components will benefit both the organization as a whole, and your existing directors. [**FACTOR 4, 9, 10**].

Don't be afraid to revisit those foundational concepts each year. You could present this annually or ask your board members to make short presentations on what these concepts mean to them. That way, you can be sure everyone is on the same page and each still understands why they continue to serve on the board.

ICK FACTOR 4: POOR COMMUNICATION

ICK FACTOR 9: LACK OF A CLEAR STRATEGY

ICK FACTOR 10: INEFFECTIVE OR MISSING ANNUAL PERFORMANCE REVIEWS, FEEDBACK, AND ASSESSMENTS

I stopped furiously scribbling notes and looked up at Kathy. "This really makes a lot of sense. I can see how it would make a difference at our board and committee meetings. I'm just a little concerned that it would make us feel very corporate or bureaucratic, and our existing board may have some push back."

"Change is always difficult Sue, especially when you've been doing things the same way for a long time. The key is to make sure the board understands why you are making these changes, and, that it is in the best interest of Second Chance. If it is handled well, the board will quickly see that the benefits of this approach greatly out-weigh any downside.

Keep in mind, *top-shelf* directors will not remain on your board if the meetings are tedious or ineffective. They have plenty of other nonprofit options for community service, so well-run, efficient and effective meetings are a necessity, not a bonus."

I sat back for a moment. "I have a pretty good idea of where I think Second Chance needs to go and what things need to look like when we finally get there, but I do see one problem. How do I raise this up to the board knowing that some will feel threatened or that this is unnecessary?"

"Good question Sue. Let's switch gears here and talk about implementation and how you can put all this into place. You're not only the leader here, but also the founder. Yes, these are tough things to deal with, but you have the best vantage point to see when things are going right and when they aren't, and when they are breaking down or you can see trouble down the road. No one has the broad and deep perspective you have. If you don't have "standing" or a right to bring important issues to the board, then no one does.

You'll need to be brave and tactful, yet compelling and unwavering, when you explain this to your board. But if you have even half the passion for Second Chance that I believe you do, I am confident you can rise to the occasion, find the right words, and build a compelling case for change."

"Thanks Kathy, I appreciate your confidence. What is the best way to prepare for this kind of meeting? How can I explain to the board that everything we've been doing needs to be reviewed and some of it probably needs to be changed to move forward in the best way?"

"Let me give you a couple suggestions. First off, when you first bring this up, keep the conversation based on facts. Don't get into any personal issues involving director performance, or a lack thereof, even if there may be some valid points to make.

It won't help your case since they will see it as a personal attack. Just focus on facts and issues that you know are true, and those where you have evidence to back up your position. Try to address important issues and problems you all face as leaders of Second Chance, board and staff. This creates common ground which you can build from later.

There will be another time and place to address any individual director challenges, and their service for Second Chance, but this is not it.

Position yourself as being one with the directors, with all of you facing these issues together, not as someone attacking the board, or worse yet, judging the board. Try to reinforce your partnership and friendship with them rather than creating defensive adversaries who feel alienated from the agency,.

It's important that you collect whatever credible data you can, to build your case. You may want to talk to other Executive Directors you know, who have already done this and find out what technique worked for them.

When you're ready, you should begin with your Executive Committee and review your thoughts, concerns, and the evidence you've developed. Some examples of evidence that may help convince them that change is needed can include:

1. Comparative data between your agency and those similar.

2.Comparative historical data about your agency. Compare current results to those from the past when things were working well.

3. Illustrate the drop in the organization's effectiveness .

4. Provide examples of what no longer works effectively or ways you may be working against your purpose.

5. Suggest an organizational assessment or a board assessment, to determine whether everyone's on the same page.

My anxiety was beginning to grow. "I have to admit, I'm a little concerned about this approach Kathy. These are not only my friends but also my bosses and it sounds a little too corporate, business-like, or legal, compared to how we normally do things. I'm afraid this just might turn them off and then I'll have real problems on my hands."

Kathy was encouraging. "Sue, remember, your board trusts you, in fact they love you. When you sit down with them, and slowly and clearly lay out a heart-felt case for change they will listen carefully. In all likelihood they will go along with your opinion and recommendations.

In fact, you've already laid the groundwork for more significant change. They've participated in a board retreat and approved a brand-new Strategic Plan for the future. Certainly they understand and recognize changes will have to come, in order to achieve the requirements of the new Strategic Plan.

In fact, they may even be sitting at home wondering how the new strategy is all going to be accomplished, just waiting for you to lead them.

Of course they will have questions, and they may have reservations, but they have trusted you and your judgment all along so there is little reason to worry they won't trust your judgment now.

Just remember, keep your reasons for change based on issues, and facts, not on people, personalities, or any individuals. The truth is, these changes are needed because the working environment, the economy, and your clients needs have changed.

Much as a golfer has to change clubs as he or she progresses down the fairway so too organizations need to periodically change the tools and operations they use to effectively serve their clients.

One suggestion I would have is for you to identify which board members would be most receptive to the changes you anticipate and then speak with them to get their support. Call them, meet with them, take them to lunch—whatever you need to do to lock them in.

Think of it as creating your own "Transition Coalition". They will help you get this through the board for approval, and will become key players in implementing the changes needed.

You can do this, Sue! The board would expect you to do this.

Author Max De Pree said, *"The first responsibility of a leader is to define reality."* No one can do it as well as you because you are the most informed and they trust you."

Kathy paused for a moment, then sat back in her chair. "How will you help Joey and his family, and others just like them, if you don't make these tough changes now? Don't they deserve your best effort?"

My mind flashed back to that morning at Second Chance and I remembered the picture Joey drew. *They* were the reason I was doing this, and I couldn't give up now.

"Thanks Kathy. That perspective was exactly what I needed. I know this will be a challenge, but it's definitely worth it."

§

In the weeks that followed, I met with a few of my board members one-on-one to discuss my concerns and ideas. I factually laid out my case for change and was patient while I let them ask me questions, challenge my thinking, and push back whenever they did not initially agree with me.

It wasn't always easy, but I knew I had to stay as open-minded as possible, and not get defensive, since any indication I was unwilling to have my thoughts challenged and questioned would come across as closed-minded and likely defeat my efforts.

Fortunately, I was able to convince them we needed to make changes. They got on board, and I was able to build my Transition Coalition.

§

Following those initial meetings, I had the tough conversation with my Executive Committee and then with the entire board. I worked hard to develop and present the data that validated my concerns about the current state of Second Chance, and the challenges we were facing. It was a very sobering meeting—no small talk or side conversations this time.

Much to my relief, the board understood what I was trying to communicate and was open to all of my thoughts regarding the changes needed at Second Chance. In fact they agreed with virtually everything I mentioned. I think all my leg work preparing some key directors in advance helped a great deal.

I was excited about how well things went with the board. It wasn't nearly as hard or confrontational as I thought it might be. This energized me even more to move forward.

I knew all this was still only part of taking Second Chance to the next level. In my heart I knew the overall momentum at Second Chance and on the board would pick up quickly and I wanted to be ready to lead in this new environment.

I called Kathy to report on how my meeting went and asked her for suggestions on improving my leadership. Second Chance needed more than I was currently providing and I wanted to step up to the new challenge.

No doubt about it, I had to raise the bar on my own performance and would need some guidance on how to take myself to the next level and bring Second Chance and its staff forward as well.

I looked forward to my next conversation with Kathy.

I.F.

ICK FACTORS — CHAPTER 10

Following are the ICK FACTORS specifically mentioned in the chapter. For a complete listing of ICK FACTORS, along with suggestions for how to Break Through these challenges and other helpful resources, please visit section two of the book.

2. NOT DELEGATING AUTHORITY, TASKS OR PROJECTS

4. POOR COMMUNICATION

5. A CULTURE WITHOUT A SENSE OF RESPONSIBILITY AND ACCOUNTABILITY

6. DISENGAGED BOARD OR INDIVIDUAL DIRECTORS

7. BOARD MEMBERS WHO DON'T DELIVER

8. INEFFECTIVE MEETINGS

9. LACK OF A CLEAR STRATEGY

10. INEFFECTIVE OR MISSING ANNUAL PERFORMANCE REVIEWS, FEEDBACK, AND ASSESSMENTS

11

LEADING THE ORGANIZATION

The next week, with cappuccinos and pumpkin scones in tow, I arrived at Kathy's office again. I had learned how to create a plan for the organization, how to help my board become more effective, and now it was time for me to step up my own game.

"Hi Sue! Are you ready to focus on Leadership today?"

"Definitely! I feel like we've made a lot of progress in terms of Strategic Planning, and developing a better board, but I'm really looking forward to seeing how I personally can help Second Chance be more successful."

"Great Sue. We will start with the six areas of an organization that the leader 'owns'. If you don't pay close attention to these areas, the organization will never reach its true potential, and could even fail. I don't mean to imply that the board and everyone else is off the hook on these areas, not at all, but these are areas that the leader must personally embrace and keep in mind, especially in the unique role as the public face of the organization.

As you make decisions, set budgets, objectives, and recruit

staff, volunteers, and board members, focusing on these six areas will have the most impact on your success.

Best-selling leadership/management author Peter Drucker, once warned about culture:

"Culture eats strategy for breakfast."

To implement your changes, and to successfully own these six areas, you will have to address the culture at Second Chance. This is the most comprehensive way to implement change, and see that it is embraced and carried out, throughout the organization. Otherwise, your existing culture will likely undermine all your new efforts and cause them to fail. The six areas are as follows:

Six Pillars for a Successful Culture Shift

1. Mission/Vision/Values–where the organization is headed, what its role is, and the ground rules the agency follows. We talked about these at length before so I don't want to repeat them except to say it's your job to be sure the agency, the board, staff and volunteers all act in alignment with the mission, vision, and values.

2. Strategy–avoid getting caught up in the details of day-to-day activity. Keep your eye on where things are headed. Leaders who take their eye off the ball or forget where the agency is headed, lose track of their key strategies. It's up to the leader to be sure the organization focuses on the strategies that have evolved out of the mission and vision discussions.

3. Strategic execution—great strategy goes nowhere without

great execution. A leader's job is to keep the resources and activity in line with the plan and strategic objectives to ensure they get done. The culture of your organization can overtake the implementation of your strategic initiatives and then you will be dead in the water. Remember the Peter Drucker quote I mentioned earlier.

4. People—a leader's job is to find the best people who would meet the needs of the agency going forward—board, staff, and volunteers. I would include key community partnerships in this section as well. What individuals or organizations in the community might qualify as outstanding Partners for Second Chance? They should be identified, tested, and then recruited onto the Second Chance team.

5. Accountability–it's the leader's job to be certain everyone does what they have agreed to do. Whether an employee, a volunteer, or a board member, everyone needs to understand that others will be relying on them to honor their commitments.

6. Measurements–the saying is *what matters gets measured and what's measured gets improved*, so leaders need to identify the key factors that will lead to success to reach that next level of service, and then consistently monitor those factors.

Also, let's talk a bit more about Strategic Execution. This is a really important thing to remember, and where many organizations fail, both nonprofit and for profit businesses. The best way to keep everything on track is to be sure you have *alignment* in your organization.""

Kathy redrew the Alignment Model she showed me a few weeks ago. Remember this chart? Hopefully, it will make much more sense to you now after our discussions. Let me summarize a bit.

In order to stay focused on your Strategic Plan and goals, avoid mission creep, and to use all your resources–people cash, time, and networking opportunities–effectively, this chart illustrates *alignment*.

GOAL ALIGNED MODEL

It all starts with your vision, mission, and values. Once you have those items firmly established and understood, you develop a few key strategies to get from where you currently are to your envisioned future. Most successful organizations have between three and five strategies at any one time. Any more than that and people get confused and overwhelmed.

These key strategies are supported by very specific goals. Your goals need to be clear and concise — SMART goals liked we discussed earlier. Remember, SMART stands for Specific, Measurable, Achievable, Realistic, and Time bound.

Every goal should be assigned to someone and each goal should have a specific deadline. As a leader you want to have periodic reports from everyone on how they're progressing in accomplishing their goals.

This is another place leaders sometimes struggle. Goals are created and get assigned to someone but there's very little follow-up along the way, or accountability when things go wrong. Good leaders know how their staff is progressing in achieving key goals and strategies.

The next section flowing from the mission-vision-values, is the type of individuals that you hire as paid staff, or recruit as volunteers or board members. It's important to create and maintain the kind of organizational culture you want, and to develop the appropriate training and orientation programs so your staff reflects the values of the organization, and stays laser focused on your mission and vision.

The same holds true for any external partners and collaborators. Any outside resources or partners you use need to fully understand your mission and vision, and respect and live your values, just like another employee.

Closely tied to your culture and strategies is your board and rules of governance. Those rules define how you operate and processes. It's important that they reflect and support your mission and vision as well.

For instance, how would it be if one of your values was honesty or truthfulness but your board or staff avoided bringing problems and difficult situations to your attention? That would not be living out the values of the agency. It's important to re-enforce the values by recruiting people onto your team who will respect the values and act accordingly. When you see someone not living up to the values, it has to be addressed directly.

Finally, when you go public through your advertising, marketing, and branding efforts, you'll want a consistent message, accurately reflecting not only what you say, but also how you act. The best advertising and public communication program cannot help an agency that does a poor job executing on its mission.

A famous marketing company CEO once said;

'Great marketing cannot help a bad product succeed, it can only help it fail quicker.'

The second point I want to make about Strategic Execution, is the potential for failure. I cannot emphasize this point strongly enough. *Most plans fail because of poor implementation.* That falls on the leader. And I'm talking about execution by everyone—staff, volunteers, and the board.

A study was done of a variety of businesses using Strategic Plans. The study found that 90% of those companies failed to execute the strategy. Pretty unbelievable, huh?

The reasons given were well within the control of leadership but were either ignored or handled poorly. They included:

- Only 25% of the managers and their incentives went to the overall strategy
- 60% of the organizations did not link budgets to the strategy
- 85% of the teams spent less than one hour a month discussing the strategy
- Only 5% of the workforce understood the strategy

So it's pretty clear Strategy, Vision, and Mission will "leak" if not frequently reinforced by the leaders.

§

Another reference point to track your organization's effectiveness and plan implementation, is how well you are serving your clients. Good leaders always listen to their client. Whether leading a retail store, manufacturing company, or anything else, it's critical to understand what your client thinks of the goods or services you provide, and how well they serve the clients' needs. A nonprofit is no different. It is healthy to evaluate if you are really impacting your client group.

Successful nonprofits should periodically check in with their clients and evaluate their operating environment to determine whether the services they currently offer are the services the client actually needs. It's so easy to just keep working harder and harder, year after year, delivering the same services, and fail to realize that today's client needs something else, or something more.

Successful leaders obsess over what they need to do *today so today's* clients can succeed in *today's* environment. It's important to get feedback whenever and wherever you can from clients, volunteers, donors, and others in the community—like foundations and key strategic partner—can all be very good sources of feedback.

Some leaders also refer to this as *Management by Walking Around*, or, *High Touch Leadership*, because it's a quick and effective way to keep an eye on things and be aware of what's happening in the agency at the grassroots level." Kathy paused for a moment and leaned back in her chair. "Sue, can you see this being helpful at Second Chance?"

I leaned forward. "It's really making a lot of sense! When we created the agency we felt we knew what our clients needed and built the organization around those needs. But, as we became busier and more focused, we never went back to see if there were other services we should be providing or to evaluate whether our existing services were as helpful as we thought they were. We may actually not be giving our clients what they need today."

Kathy nodded. "Another point to consider—and I know you may not like to hear this—but what if you determined that another nearby nonprofit agency does a better job at something than you do? What would you do then?"

"Hmm… I had never even thought about that…"

"Well, if that ever were the case, you might want to collaborate with them and let them handle what they do best and let Second Chance take on other services you do the best."

I agreed that made sense in theory, but the thought of giving up one of our programs was something we would not do lightly. Kathy understood my reservations and asked me to at least keep that idea in the back of my head. She pointed out that sometimes the best use of our resources is to exit a program so we could put our limited resources into a program we do very well.

She took a sip of her cappuccino and continued, "So far we've talked mainly about leading the organization. Let's change gears at this point and discuss leading volunteers. Successful nonprofit leaders know how to identify, recruit, and lead high-impact volunteers. This is one of those areas of nonprofit leadership where successful leaders really earn their stripes.

It's one thing to have an adequate number of volunteers helping you accomplish your normal, everyday, workflow issues. But what I'm talking about is finding the high-impact volunteers who have special skills that they want to offer the nonprofit. These skills could be in the areas of marketing, finance, relationship-development, or technology. Smart leaders are always on the lookout for people with unique skills, who are willing to donate time to the agency.

Often nonprofit leaders make a huge mistake right up front, in the initial interview with a new volunteer. Rarely are volunteers interviewed and asked what special skills, talents or connections they might bring. Instead, they are just assigned to an area needing the most help at that moment. This can be huge waste of talent. [**FACTOR 3, 4**]

ICK FACTOR 3: WEAK VOLUNTEER ORIENTATION AND MANAGEMENT

ICK FACTOR 4: POOR COMMUNICATION

Remember, volunteers come with various motivations to help

you, and they can come and go as they please. Try to find out what attracted them to your agency and what specifically they'd like to contribute. Among their motivations may be:

1. Doing something they love
2. Giving back to the community–making a difference
3. A deep passion for the cause
4. A desire to meet new people
5. Wanting to learn new skills

Smart leaders remember that all volunteers are there because they want to be there not because have to be. It's important to respect and celebrate your volunteers frequently.

There are several different categories of volunteers, and out of respect for them, and to help them become as valuable as possible to the agency and your clients, it's a good idea to determine how they can best fit in to your organization. [**FACTOR 3**]

ICK FACTOR 3: WEAK VOLUNTEER ORIENTATION AND MANAGEMENT

Some individuals have great wisdom in certain areas that are important to the agency. Others simply want to get their hands dirty and help out however needed. They will do just about anything. Still others are great community ambassadors and know a lot of individuals. They can help open doors that otherwise would have been closed to you. They also make great external representatives. Finally, there are others that are in a position to make significant financial donations.

The key thing to remember is everyone has special skills and a special motivation to be there and it's the smart leader that taps into these skills and motivations and finds the best way to engage that volunteer to create a mutually transforming experience."

"That makes a lot of sense. I can see where we've done some things well with our volunteers, but others are definitely lacking. What else should I know about becoming a better leader for Second Chance?"

"Let me leave you with some final thoughts I've picked up along the way. Think of these as leadership lessons to live by. Successful nonprofit leaders:

• Have the trust of their staff. Trust promotes communication and allows for frank and open discussions, including conflict resolution.

• Understand that accountability goes all the way up, down, and across an organization. No one is immune.

• Measure, assess, and evaluate periodically. Whether it's individual performance reviews, board self-assessment, or individual board members being evaluated, these open, honest, and frank discussions are good for the agency and good for the individual. Successful leaders know this and see to it that the agency is regularly reviewed and evaluated.

• Understand that sometimes they have to say "No"

• Reinforce the Mission, Vision, Values and key strategies frequently.

• Establish clear roles and responsibilities through written job descriptions, organizational charts, annual goals, and frequent communication.

• Invest in the organization's infrastructure. Do not be overly obsessed with the Nonprofit Overhead Myth that says one must keep administration and fundraising expenses to some arbitrary low percentage of overall revenue. Instead, strike a balance between incurring expenses, and investments that lead to sustainability.

• Participate in professional development programs, such as reading books, lifelong learning opportunities, Advisory Councils, Peer Groups, Mastermind Groups, and many other inexpensive executive development programs.

• Successful leaders never fear challenging the status quo, their operating model, or themselves.

I know it's a lot to take in, but if you want to help lead Second Chance in a new and better direction, these things are vital to moving forward."

I sat there amazed at all I had been learning through these sessions, and all I had begun to accomplish at Second Chance by starting to use these new methods. No wonder I had been struggling before I started working with Kathy.

I was slowly feeling my passion return and I became more determined than ever to turn things around at Second Chance. I was committed to becoming the leader I needed to be, to lead our organization to that "next level" of impact.

As I packed up my things, Kathy offered to meet with me on occasion to serve as a sounding board and to coach me through any tough spots, providing encouragement as needed. I readily accepted Kathy's offer and thanked her again for all her help.

§

Walking to the car I realized I needed to get my thoughts together and come up with a high level list of the things I needed to accomplish based on all I had learned from Kathy. I headed back to my favorite coffee shop, found a quiet spot in the corner, and pulled out my notebook.

As I created my list I gave each step a due date, then reorganized the list chronologically. This gave me a convenient map, and a timeline, with all the critical steps I would need to take, making it much easier for me to track progress and stay on task when things got a little confusing or I ran into resistance.

When I was done I took a deep breath. There was a lot on the list, but it was all doable, and I could really start to see Second Chance heading in a positive direction.

I.F.

ICK FACTORS – Chapter 11

Following are the ICK FACTORS specifically mentioned in the chapter along with suggestions for how to Break Through these challenges. For a complete listing of ICK FACTORS and other helpful resources, please visit the back of the book.

3. WEAK VOLUNTEER ORIENTATION AND MANAGEMENT

4. POOR COMMUNICATION

12

MAKING PROGRESS

Over the next several months I got down to work, and the more progress I made the more energized I became. It even got easier. While I was busier than ever before I could see progress being made every week. Some weeks a lot of progress, some weeks just a little, but I kept things moving in the right direction and never wavered.

I met with the Executive Committee and we all came to an agreement on the profile and skill sets of future director candidates that might best help Second Chance accomplish the Strategic Plan.

I began compiling a list of potential candidates who had these skills, connections, resources, etc. by leveraging the networks of my current board. We decided on the most desirable skills/talents for Second Chance's current board of directors. The list included:

- Wisdom/life experience
- Good judgment
- Strategic thinking
- Marketing skills
- Financial acumen

- Someone whose friends and network include generous donors
- Representatives of the grocery store and clothing store industries

Before long we had identified several potential candidates and created a list of those we felt best fit our immediate needs. The Executive Committee and I began the process of reaching out and recruiting a few of the top candidates to determine their interest.

The one thing I worried most about never really happened. I had been concerned the current board would resist the changes and adding new directors, taking these as signs they were no longer helpful or wanted. Above all, I hadn't wanted them to feel used and then cast aside just as things were starting to pick up.

This was a big concern for me almost from the beginning since I appreciated each of the original board members and all they had done. I didn't want to jeopardize any relationships, or create any controversy in our community, but I knew things had to change, even at the board level, if Second Chance was to evolve and thrive.

After all my preparations, when I sat down with the board to go over all of these things, the right words just came to me when I needed them the most.

I even caught a big break when a quick review of our bylaws revealed I could have up to 10 directors on the board. This gave me room to add a few new candidates without needing any current directors to resign. That made things a lot easier.

I caught another unexpected break when I realized these new directors were used to getting things done—planning, execution, accountability—and understood how to run successful organizations. I began to see a shift in our culture and slowly things began to change for the better.

In addition to their individual skills, these directors brought a sense of service, and a sense of accountability, pace, and execution to their board service and the culture in general. This made some of my friends on the board rethink their commitment and ultimately decide to step off of the board. There were no hard feelings, they could see things were headed in a new direction and felt it was probably time for them to give someone else a chance on the board.

Friendships remained strong and the directors who resigned committed to volunteering in the future from time to time.

I also began working on my own personal leadership style. It wasn't easy and initially I struggled with giving up some of my duties and delegating them to others. It was hard to ultimately be responsible for everything, are then to give authority to someone else.

Letting go was very difficult, but it was one of the best things I've done. Initially I'd been convinced the whole operation would collapse if I didn't keep my fingers in every pie. I knew if we were to grow, I had to take things off of my plate and give them to someone else. I had to give others a chance to grow as well.

What surprised me most was how great it felt to empower others to take on new and more important duties, freeing

Spending an occasional afternoon volunteering there was life-giving to me. It made me a better leader when I saw how the staff and volunteers had everything covered so I could focus on those strategic activities best handled by me.

§

Several months after our planning session -- Frank, our Strategic Planning facilitator -- referred a friend of his ,Bill, to me. Bill had recently retired as sales rep and wanted to start giving back to the community. When he asked Frank for a recommendation, I was honored that he mentioned Second Chance.

Bill and I met and hit it off immediately. He was tired of chasing the almighty dollar and wanted to do something that was meaningful for people, aside from just posting good sales number each quarter.

One introductory tour through our food pantry and clothing closet and he was hooked. He wanted to volunteer up to three days a week, whenever special meetings, appointments, or events, dictated.

I had never thought of my role in seeking food, clothing, and cash donations as being a sales job. I just approached people, hat in hand, asking for their help. But this guy was unbelievable. He put together a list of talking points about Second Chance, much as he had in his prior jobs, outlining all the benefits to the community and to others by supporting us.

I have to say his approach made me just a little uncomfortable until I heard him speak to a prospective donor about why they should support the work we were doing, and how they would feel if they joined us in our work. He was terrific and soon became our part-time, paid Development Director. Together, we came up with a marketing and development strategy that really helped us, and even included a successful foray into the world of social media and online marketing.

§

Twelve months after Bill joined us we moved into our our new facility and it is awesome! Bill knew a property manager/neighbor of his who found some vacant warehouse/office space which is working out perfectly for us. It was located close to our original facility and very close to public transportation, which is a big help to our clients. We also added two new programs for our clients—computer training and job search assistance. We are currently on track to double our cash donations and in-kind gifts within five years and have almost 50 volunteers!

As I reflect back, I can definitely see this all didn't randomly fall into place or just happen. I had to recognize we needed to do things differently in order to get different results. I had to step up, make some hard choices, and have a few difficult conversations, but it was all worth it.

13

TWELVE MONTHS LATER

"It was the best of times, it was the worst of times…"
— Charles Dickens

It is hard to describe how fast the last twelve months came and went. I was busier than I had ever been but also more energized. I had removed myself from much of my previous day-to-day activities and transferred many of my previous responsibilities to others. I see now how investing my time and energy more strategically, only in those activities that I should do, or where it made the most sense for the benefit of Second Chance and our clients, was making a big impact on the organization.

At first it was really hard letting go of all those things I loved to do like handing out food and clothing to our clients, visiting with them as they stood in line, or going around town looking for food and clothing donations. But I had a very strong team of volunteers and staff who welcomed the chance to take over more and more of our activities so I could focus on things that were critical for my role.

I did occasionally take the time to work in the food pantry.

me up to focus on my key responsibilities—things that only I could or should do.

I was beginning to get it, to understand all Kathy had been teaching me. If Second Chance was to succeed and ultimately sustain itself long term, I had to start thinking less as the founder and more as a leader. A leader who was accountable to the board and the community for Second Chance's well-being.

It was definitely easier said than done, but as things progressed and I saw how we were growing bigger, stronger, and making a greater impact in the community, I was able to let go more and more, and let others play a role in leadership and decision-making.

14

EPILOGUE

It is late on a Tuesday morning and I'm headed off to a lunch meeting with a new potential donor. As I walk through our waiting area I see several people waiting to meet with our staff. I smile at one woman and she smiles back, exhaustion on her face, but hope in her eyes. My eyes rest on a framed picture above our reception desk. It's the picture Joey drew not so long ago. Below it is one sentence, stenciled in script lettering. The words read:

Welcome to Second Chance — A Community Bringing Hope and Assistance to the Those in Need.

I still think about Joey—with the big, blue eyes, and his mom. They are the ones that got me started on this road of change and sustainability. My role has completely changed. My days look nothing like they used to.

We are serving more people than I ever imagined, and I am as excited and passionate as I have ever been. I owe it all to that little boy and his mom. They reminded me why I started Second Chance and what I believe I was called to do. *I will never forget them.*

Part 2:
Overcoming
The ICK FACTORS

I.F.

THE ICK FACTORS

Break Through is a story illustrating some of the most common issues and problems facing many nonprofits every day. These challenges can paralyze a leader or board if not handled well. Many of them keep nonprofits from getting to the next level and making a more significant impact.

Throughout the story you may have even recognized a few of these challenges in your own agency. **ICK FACTORS** can make nonprofit leadership a bigger challenge than it needs to be.

Some **ICK FACTORS** may not look like problems at first but eventually, by avoiding them, delaying their handling, or choosing the wrong strategy, they can cause huge headaches, friction, and even more problems down the road.

The suggestions that follow were designed to help you understand, diagnose, and Break Through these **ICK FACTORS** in your own organization.

1

NON-STRATEGIC BOARD CANDIDATE SOURCING

UNDERSTANDING THE ICK FACTOR

Some boards are just not put together in a way that gives the organization its best chance to succeed. No one can doubt the motivation, desire, and dedication of board members. Their hearts are in the right place and they want to serve. However, if an organization is to accomplish its mission, it also needs the right directors—directors whose skills, experiences, talents, and networks match up with the needs of the organization.

HOW CAN YOU BREAK THROUGH?

With a Strategic Plan in hand, the board's composition should be reviewed. There are tools available to help governance committees shape a board that gives the organization its best chance to succeed. This function should not be taken lightly or under artificial deadlines. It is far better to keep one or more open board seats unfilled until the right candidates become available than to just fill them with anyone.

Some organizations maintain a list of qualified board candidates all year long so they can be recruited, evaluated, and brought on as needed. One cannot be too careful here or take this as a part- time responsibility. Everyone should always be on the lookout for qualified candidates who may become available and who have an interest in the organization's mission.

In addition to serving as a fiduciary, another part of a board's responsibility is to provide the Executive Director with feedback and advice as necessary. A well-rounded and skilled board can do this effectively. Unless the board has been built strategically, this tremendous opportunity may be lost.

No Executive Director should miss the opportunity to leverage his or her board's expertise for the benefit of the mission.

2

NOT DELEGATING AUTHORITY AND TASKS OR PROJECTS

UNDERSTANDING THE ICK FACTOR

They say leadership is a lonely role and it can be, but some leaders make it a lot lonelier than necessary. A few leaders, especially founders, believe in their hearts that no one understands what needs to be done or how to do it as well as they do. Quite understandably, the organization becomes an extension of them. Nevertheless, this kind of thinking creates real problems.

When leaders do not habitually delegate tasks or projects to others who are capable of handling them, they not only bog themselves down with low value activity at the expense of more critical things, but they signal to the staff that they are either not trusted or incapable. This can be terribly damaging to morale and culture.

While the leader may feed his or her ego with feelings of self-importance through this busyness, the high value staff and volunteers are thinking it may be time to go elsewhere to grow, learn, and develop.

There is an African proverb that says, *"If you want to go fast, go alone. If you want to go far, go together."*

HOW CAN YOU BREAK THROUGH?

There are three types of activities for Executive Directors. The first are the important things that only the leader can do—no one else. Then there are the tasks that no Executive Director should ever do. Those should always be delegated to someone else, with all the authority necessary. Finally, there are those tasks or projects that may be delegated. Whenever possible, they should be given to someone else to complete, along with the necessary authority and information to get them done.

Think how powerful the message of trust and confidence you send, when you empower another to do something beyond their normal job. This is real professional development at its best. It's also a great way to develop and retain your key performers.

While delegation may feel uncomfortable at first, and it often does, it is one of a leader's most powerful tools and should be used as much as possible.

3

WEAK VOLUNTEER ORIENTATION AND MANAGEMENT

UNDERSTANDING THE ICK FACTOR

Volunteers are always appreciated but sometimes they are taken for granted. They should be treated just as well as paid staff. After all, in addition to doing their valuable work they are helping hold down costs. That's why they are called volunteers. Most nonprofits would be out of business without them. It is important to give them the same level of respect and attention shown others.

HOW CAN YOU BREAK THROUGH?

One way is to meet with them periodically to hear what they have to say. Since they are often in the trenches delivering the services provided, they have a unique perspective and may have some great ideas on how things could be done better, etc.

Whenever possible, at their first offer to join the organization, interview them and assign them to a place where their service heart is, if at all possible. Just assigning them haphazardly to your tasks, projects or activities needing the most help may not be their best use. Find out what makes them tick and how they'd like to serve. Then, if possible, put them in that position and watch them shine. See Chapter 11 regarding leading volunteers.

4

POOR COMMUNICATION

UNDERSTANDING THE ICK FACTOR

Poor communication, or not communicating at all, is often the cause of many problems. Most of these problems probably would never have arisen in the first place, but because of a reluctance to address them, a hope that they will simply go away, or not finding the right words to introduce the topic, they are never addressed head on. This allows them to fester and contaminate the board room.

HOW CAN YOU BREAK THROUGH?

It's usually best to address these issues head-on and resolve them as they arise. They only get worse and more complicated the longer they hang on, and will soon be like a cloud over the board.

Avoidance is not the only way poor communication damages organizations. Another more subtle, yet equally damaging way, is when leaders hold back important information, or their opinions, on important issues. This lack of transparency leads to distrust and once peoples' motivations are in question, the damage is almost irreparable. Without trust and openness in the boardroom, little can be accomplished.

One way to address this is to think through the conversation— or presentation if in front of the board—ahead of time so you are sure you have chosen the right words, thereby minimizing the chance of anxiety and defensiveness on everyone's part. Think of it as building a smooth on-ramp into the topic so your audience and you remain united and on common ground in addressing the problem you have tossed onto the table.

Figuratively speaking, act as if you and your audience are all sitting on the same side of the discussion table looking at the problem together, shoulder to shoulder, as a shared problem needing a solution, rather than sitting on opposite sides of the table, in an adversarial negotiations session. You cannot control how people will react, but you can position the discussions as collaborative and open. How they ultimately handle things is up to them, but anticipating trouble should not stop a leader from doing the right thing.

Generally, it is a wise practice for the Executive Director and the board chair to speak periodically to each other between meetings, so everyone is kept up to date on important issues. No surprises is one of the best communication rules of thumb.

If the problem involves just one individual, it is best to address it with the individual personally to get to the cause (and then the solution) of the friction.

An effective resource with many tools and suggestions to help with how to address and resolve communication problems is Crucial Conversations, by Kerry Patterson and Joseph Grenny.

5

A CULTURE WITHOUT A SENSE OF RESPONSIBILITY AND ACCOUNTABILITY

UNDERSTANDING THE ICK FACTOR

An organizational culture that passively accepts when individuals (staff, board, leadership, volunteers) do not deliver on what they promised, is a culture that can lead to ineffectiveness, a lack of impact, and the loss of high value staff and board members. High performing people will not stick around when others are not pulling their weight or delivering on promises.

In the short term, some high performers will step up and cover for others, but eventually they will leave and join another board. Remember, other boards and Executive Directors are always working to recruit great board candidates onto their boards, so it is critical to make board service with you valuable and enjoyable to them—not a burden.

HOW CAN YOU BREAK THROUGH?

There are several ways to hold people accountable, even in nonprofit work, and you'll have to figure out which ones work best in your organizational culture and with your personal leadership style. One way is to be absolutely clear on what is expected and by when. Clear meeting minutes capturing all agreements and assignments made, and what parameters were set, can be very helpful.

Another way to help hold people accountable, is to set the standard upfront and consistently that while no one likes bad news or unmet expectations, it is important leadership is kept current on the progress of projects and goals. The earlier problems are identified, the earlier they can be resolved, especially problems that could cause delays or additional work later on.

It may be best to have a private conversation with someone who consistently misses deadlines or fails to meet his/her responsibilities to learn why this problem persists. It may be fixable.

During board meetings, it should be clear that everyone is relying on each other or a committee to get certain things done on time. When delays appear inevitable or actually do occur, a revised timetable or approach should be established right away. Simply overlooking someone's consistent failure to deliver is a bad habit to form and will send the wrong message to everyone else.

6

DISENGAGED BOARD OR INDIVIDUAL DIRECTORS

UNDERSTANDING THE ICK FACTOR

No matter how hard you try, you always run the risk of taking on a board member who seems to be along for the ride and is not pulling his/her weight. Or worse yet, a couple of the board members lay low and just show up for meetings unprepared, uninformed, and listless. But worst of all, is an active board member who suddenly goes into cruise control and pulls back. In all three cases, the leader, the organization, and the board all needlessly suffer.

HOW CAN YOU BREAK THROUGH?

The best way to avoid this problem is to keep it from surfacing in the first place. Often this can be accomplished through a clear, straightforward discussion with each new director candidate about the organizations' expectations for individuals serving on the board. This is the time to be certain the board candidate understands the role and is willing to put in the necessary time to do the job the right way.

When it does occur, see [**FACTOR 1**] above. It is time for a conversation with that individual to find out what is going on in his/her life. There may be a way to salvage a great board member but you will never find out if you don't try.

A disengaged board may suggest there are problems between the Executive Director and several directors. They may be personality or style-related or they may be related to direction of the organization. In this case, a private conversation between the board chair and Executive Director, or others as the case may be, can be the best option to get to the bottom of the friction.

If one of the organization's values is truthfulness, honesty, integrity, openness, mutual respect, etc. then it is altogether proper to remind those involved that they in order to live up to values they created or accepted when they joined the board, a conversation is warranted. Often, that can help open the discussions.

One last point. Sometimes people are uncomfortable bringing up tough issues, but it may be possible to get them to speak through a confidential board assessment. These confidential tools are great at smoking out whatever is going on with the board and leadership. Directors can be open and frank without feeling like they are attacking someone when they complete the assessment privately and all responses are aggregated for analysis.

7

BOARD MEMBERS WHO DON'T DELIVER

UNDERSTANDING THE ICK FACTOR

Too many directors are asked onto a nonprofit board without a clear understanding of what their role and responsibilities are, and what is expected of them as a director. They show up at meetings and just sit there for many months before figuring out what they think they should do. This is terribly unfair to them, the board, and the organization.

Every board candidate should have a chance to understand what their role would be and specifically what he or she is being recruited onto the board to do. This gives both sides a chance to determine how good a fit the candidate will be before any commitments are made. After all, once someone is on the board, they are likely going to be there for a long time.

HOW CAN YOU BREAK THROUGH?

One tool that successful organizations use is a Board Orientation and Training Manual. Typically, these manuals are unique to each organization but often contain similar information. By developing this manual over time and keeping it updated, a board can provide its members and candidates with critical information so they can serve effectively and fully understand what is expected of them.

8

INEFFECTIVE MEETINGS

UNDERSTANDING THE ICK FACTOR

Nothing may hinder a well intended nonprofit quicker than conducting ineffective meetings and poorly managing time. It may also be the most effective way to lose valuable (and busy) board members who have already sat in meetings all day. Meetings must be run crisply and cover only the items a board needs or wants to know.

HOW CAN YOU BREAK THROUGH?

Almost all of the board's "heavy lifting" should be done at committee level. Committees are where issues are fully investigated, clarified, and made ready for board presentation and disposition. Once its work is done the committee makes a presentation to the entire board for its discussion and vote. If additional research is needed, the chair should quickly refer the item back to committee and move on to other matters. A committee of the whole board should only be used in rare circumstances.

9

LACK OF A CLEAR STRATEGY

UNDERSTANDING THE ICK FACTOR

Not having a strategy and a plan to carry it out is a frequent problem. A Strategic Plan provides everyone with a road map to where the organization is headed. It guides all decision-making includes who needs to be hired, where to allocate resources, what projects to take on, and basically when to say yes and when to say no. Without a plan an organization will drift and never accomplish its mission.

HOW CAN YOU BREAK THROUGH?

See Chapter 8 in the book for more information on how to create a Strategic Plan.

10

INEFFECTIVE OR MISSING ANNUAL PERFORMANCE REVIEWS, FEEDBACK, AND ASSESSMENTS

UNDERSTANDING THE ICK FACTOR

If your board is like most others, as soon as the gavel falls, usually late in the evening, everyone makes a mad dash for home. Most board members have full-time jobs and a life outside of their board service so they do not have the luxury of time to sit and just think about or discuss the organization and how it is doing.

For these reasons it makes a lot of sense to conduct annual reviews: 1) of the Executive Director by the board, 2) of board members by the board chair and Executive Director jointly, 3) of the board as a whole by the board and key leaders, and 4) of the organization by the board and key leaders.

HOW CAN YOU BREAK THROUGH?

Most people want feedback-to know how they are performing, and are willing to address any weak areas. There should be a process in place to automatically conduct reviews and assessments annually. If they are introduced unexpectedly and without proper foundation, they will surely be met with suspicion and anxiety.

Sometimes these personal reviews between directors, board chairs and the Executive Director turn into coaching sessions. Other times, they can become a great exchange of information. Either way, honest discussions about where things are and where they need to go are healthy exercises and only benefit everyone involved

The results coming out of an organizational assessment are very telling and valuable. Often, they get to the root of problems the board is experiencing but has been unwilling or unable to identify.

No matter the case, they are fast and effective ways to accurately take the temperature of the directors, see what they are thinking, and what their perceptions are. Often misunderstandings and confusion will surface and can be addressed over time. People are usually honest and frank when completing confidential surveys which is what makes this tool so valuable.

§

A NOTE FROM TOM

Sue is now off and running, implementing her Strategic Plan and making the changes Second Chance needs. Almost immediately she began to see positive change take hold and impact the entire organization. Everyone at Second Chance—the staff and volunteers, the board, and especially the clients—began reaping the benefits of Sue's focus on overcoming the ICK FACTORS of nonprofit leadership.

She will undoubtedly benefit from additional professional development, including future mentoring and coaching from Kathy, but she is already qualified, empowered and equipped to lead Second Chance where the board has decided to go over the next three years.

Sue realized she and Second Chance had to make important changes to not only survive but thrive going forward. By taking those steps they are now prepared to *do even better at doing good*" and their best days are still ahead.

Every nonprofit can benefit from these steps. All it takes is the right motivation...like a wide set of deep blue eyes...to begin the process. What will it take for you to step up?

Leading a nonprofit can be one of the most challenging and rewarding experiences for someone with a passion to help others. It will require strong character, lasting vision, and a willingness to learn and occasionally experiment with ways of doing things. It will also require you to move beyond your comfort zone, make tough decisions, and take measured chances. But I promise in the end, the rewards will far out way the effort as you learn to discover your organization's true potential.

If you are working toward achieving change in your nonprofit, please visit www.TomOkarma.com or the companion website for this book www.ICKFACTORS.com. You will find many blog articles and tools available to you, so you too can conquer your ICK FACTORS and take your organization to its next level.

I would love to hear from you on your progress, as you work towards *Leading For Impact.*

— Tom Okarma

RECOMMENDATIONS FOR FURTHER READING

The NonProfit Answer Book, Third Edition, BoardSource

Good Governance for Nonprofits, Fredric Laughin and Robert C Andringa

The One Hour Plan for Growth, Joe Calhoon

Managing the Nonprofit Organization, Principles and Practices, Peter F. Drucker

The Five Most Important Questions You will Ever Ask About Your Organization, Peter F. Drucker

Leading Change, John P Kotter

Mastering the Management Buckets, John Pearson

Leading People: Transforming Business From the Inside Out, Robert H. Rosen and Paul B. Brow

ONLINE RESOURCES

Christian Leadership Alliance
www.christianleadershipalliance.org

Evangelical Council of Financial Accountability
www.ecfa.org

Tom Okarma, www.TomOkarma.com

ACKNOWLEDGMENTS

I have many people to thank for helping me write this book. Some I worked for or volunteered with, some I spoke with and learned from, and a few wrote exceptional books giving me great inspiration and helped me carve out my own approach to leadership, strategy, and board development.

It is impossible to list them all but most of them worked or volunteered at great organizations, including:

- The Barnabas Group-Chicago
- Christian Leadership Alliance
- People's Resource Center
- Bright Hope
- Providence International Foundation
- Fox Valley Carpenter's Place
- Giving DuPage
- Orion Cap/DPIC Companies, Inc
- PLAN

I want to thank those who specifically helped me with the writing and production of this book. They reviewed, edited, and made many valuable suggestions along the way. Special thanks to Bob Andringa, Dan Busby, C.H. Dyer, Annette Forster, Tami Heim, Gordon Koppin, Gordon Murphy, Kathy Blair, Mary Ellen Durbin, Christa Habel March, Annette . Their keen insights and suggestions were extraordinary and greatly improved upon the original manuscript.

Special thanks to, among others, Bob Andringa, John Pearson,and Joe Calhoon, authors who wrote several excellent books on this subject matter. Also, special thanks to Sarah Bruns and her team at inGauge IQ, Inc. for book editing, design, and more.

Finally, I want to thank my wife Sue for encouraging me to take my leadership experience and skills into the nonprofit world once I left my for-profit career. She has spent many years serving nonprofits as a very effective fundraiser. She saw how my skills could be helpful in equipping others "do well at doing good".

My "Second Half" in life has a whole new energy, purpose, and direction because of her continued encouragement and belief in me and my abilities.

Thank you Sue!

§

GLOSSARY

This Glossary was designed to provide quick and easy-to-understand definitions of key terms used in the book, based on the intent of the author. Some terms may have different meanings or implications in alternate contexts.

501 (C) (3) — A section of the Internal Revenue Code describing conditions under which a nonprofit can operate free from any federal taxes.

ALIGNMENT — A term used to describe when all of an organization's assets, resources, staffing, operations, goals, etc. are fully in support of its MISSION, VISION and VALUES.

BOARD COMMITTEE — A group consisting specific members of a board, generally created to carry out specified functions, programs, or projects assigned by the board.

BOARD DEVELOPMENT — The term used to describe how an organization identifies, recruits, trains, and utilizes its directors.

BOARD OF DIRECTORS —The body of elected individuals who are legally responsible for the activities of the nonprofit organization. Specific authority, duties, and responsibilities, are contained in the organization's bylaws and all applicable state and federal laws.

BOARD POLICY MANUAL — A living document containing specific guidelines for all significant decisions and votes made by the board. While its makeup is flexible and for each board to determine, most manuals will include history, bylaws, job descriptions, strategic plans, budgets, all procedures and policy decisions, and other related items. There is no limit to what the manual may contain. Its value, however, is in using it, as well as keeping it current and relevant.

CODE OF CONDUCT POLICY — A set of ethical and moral rules, regulations, or guidelines, established by the board, describing acceptable behaviors in certain situations.

COMPENSATION POLICY — A written policy covering how the agency sets compensation for its staff—salary, benefits, etc.

CONFLICT OF INTEREST POLICY — A document confirming the board's commitment to avoid conflicts of interest, and outlining the process it will take to handle any issues if/when they arise. A conflict of interest occurs when the interests of a board member conflict with the best interests of the organization. It is best to completely avoid all conflicts of interest when possible, but on occasion they do occur. Sometimes conflicts cannot be avoided and as long as the board is aware of the conflict, approves how it should be handled, and closely monitors it, there should be no problem.

DASHBOARD REPORT TEMPLATE — A document including a list of all top priority issues with a letter grade assigned to each one, to depict the current status of the issue.

Some boards may use a red light, yellow light, green light approach. Others use a numbering system, or a thumbs up, thumbs down, or thumbs level indicator.

DONOR FATIGUE — A term describing when a nonprofit's faithful and consistent donors begin to make smaller donations, donate less frequently, or cease donations altogether. This usually occurs when donors feel excessive pressure through a nonprofit's fundraising, including requests that are viewed as too frequent and/or too pushy.

DUTY OF CARE — requiring each board member to exercise what the general public would recognize as a "reasonable" level of care in carrying out his or her duties. In other words, there is no obligation or expectation for a board member to be perfect, but he/she must act in a way such that ordinary people would expect one to act, assuming similar circumstances.

DUTY OF LOYALTY — requiring each board member to give undivided allegiance, without any conflicts of interest, when making decisions about the organization. They can never obtain personal gain from actions as a board member, and must always act in the best interest of the organization.

DUTY OF OBEDIENCE — requiring a director to remain faithful to the organization's mission, and take no action that is inconsistent with the central goals of the organization.

EMERGENCY SUCCESSION POLCY — A written policy explaining the conditions for a temporary transfer of leadership and how it is to occur, i.e, who does what going forward. In the event of a need for an emergency transfer of leadership from the CEO/Executive Director to another, this document helps keep the natural order of the nonprofit's work continuing uninterrupted during what may become confusing times.

EXPENSE REIMBURSEMENT POLICY — A written policy defining reimbursable expenses and the procedures and forms used to collect qualifying reimbursement.

FIDUCIARY DUTY — A legal duty to always act in another's best interests, in this case, the nonprofit's best interests.

GIFT ACCEPTANCE POLICY — A written policy describing what type of gifts the organization can or cannot accept. In a few cases, it will describe conditions under which it can accept certain gifts such as buildings, stock, vacant land, etc.

GOALS — A set of desired end results adopted by a nonprofit, which guide all future activities of the agency, including priorities, budgeting, staffing, operations, etc.

GOVERNANCE — The mechanism by which a nonprofit shapes how it will operate. It consists of all agreed upon procedures, policies, restrictions, authorities and responsibilities. Often these materials are kept in an updated Board Policy Manual.

GOVERNANCE COMMITTEE — A key committee of the board, it is usually responsible to see that all governing policies are fully and consistently followed. It is also charged with the initial evaluations of future board candidates to evaluate their "fit" based on the board's future needs. This committee is also responsible to see the board is properly trained, new directors receive a comprehensive orientation, and that the board conducts, and follows, its own strategic plan.

HIGH-IMPACT VOLUNTEERS — Volunteers who, based on either the effective skills they possess, or the significant way they serve at an agency, may be categorized as being in the top ten percent of volunteers.

MANAGEMENT BY WALKING AROUND (MBWA) OR HIGH TOUCH MANAGEMENT — A style of leadership which generally refers to managers spending some part of their time listening to problems and ideas of their staff, while wandering around an organization.

MEASUREMENTS/METRICS — A set of key numeric values that can be used to access an organizations progress toward a specific goal.

MISSION/MISSION STATEMENT — A statement describing the purpose of the agency and why it exists. It describes the end result of all the anticipated activities of the agency.

NONPROFIT OVERHEAD MYTH — A belief among some, that a nonprofit must do everything it can to hold down its administrative expenses or risk appearing to the public to be wasteful, bloated, or inefficient in its operations.

ORGANIZATIONAL ASSESSMENT (OR) BOARD ASSESSMENT — A general term describing a wide variety of tools that allow an organization (or board) to evaluate itself. These tools can be used to determine priorities, evaluate effectiveness, seek consensus, etc.

POSITIONING — The way a marketer attempts to carve out

a unique niche for a nonprofit in a donor's mind. It is a way to present an organization relative to others. For instance, one agency may assist unmarried pregnant teens while another one may work with unmarried teen mothers.

RISK MANAGEMENT POLICY — A written policy assessing the relative risk, or exposure-to-loss, an organization may have, and what proactive and reactive steps should be taken to avoid, lessen, accept, or transfer the risks to others. Each nonprofit's policy will be unique to its own service offerings.

SMART GOALS — Goals that are Specific, Measurable, Achievable, Realistic, and Time-bound.

STRATEGIC INITIATIVES/KEY STRATEGIES — A high-level set of priorities the organization has decided to pursue.

STRATEGY/STRATEGIC PLAN — A document describing in broad terms, where the organization is headed, along with its priorities, and intended key initiatives, to carry out its mission. It is usually composed of the following four elements: Vision/Vision Statement; Mission/Mission Statement; Values/Value Statement; Goals.

TASK FORCE — A group of individuals appointed by the board, to focus on a single issue which can often be resolved in a specific period of time. Generally a Task Force will formulate a recommendation for consideration by the board or committee which formed the Task Force.

TERM LIMITS — The length of service time a board member may serve. It is often described in two facets: number of years in a term, and how many terms a board member may serve.

TRANSITION COALITION — A group of staff members and volunteers who have accepted the need to change and are willing to actively install and reinforce those efforts throughout the organization. Every successful change process needs a transition coalition since there will invariably be forces at work to undermine or ignore the changes needed.

VALUES/VALUES STATEMENT — A high-level set of ground rules. A Values Statement describes how your organization will conduct itself as it implements its strategic plan and pursues its mission.

VISION/VISION STATEMENT — A high-level statement, or aspiration, describing what the organization or agency would ideally like to see in the future.

WORKING BOARDS — In "board language" there are working boards and governing boards. A working board is one whose reach goes beyond monitoring the end results of an organization's work, to extend to potential involvement with its means and execution.

Working boards may perform staff work and involve themselves in discussions about "how" things are done, instead of just "what" things are being done. This is often a characteristic of small or start-up nonprofits.

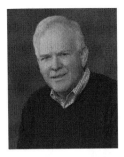

ABOUT THE AUTHOR

Tom Okarma is a product of the south side of Chicago and currently resides in the greater Chicago area. He has been a successful leader in both the nonprofit and business worlds and has led or served on a variety of boards.

He has over 30 years of varied and progressive experience in the insurance industry, rising from claims representative to small business owner to Chief Executive Officer leading a staff of 300+ employees. He also has nearly 10 years of experience working with nonprofits.

Tom helps nonprofits with effectiveness in execution, organizational excellence, Strategic Planning, change management, client intimacy, and talent management.

He has been there, done that, and learned critical lessons about successful board development and governance, Strategic Planning, and leadership. He is an approachable catalyst for senior leaders and provides senior staff members, stakeholders and boards with an understanding and discerning ear.

To learn more about Tom or read his thoughts on leadership for nonprofits, visit www.TomOkarma.com.

Made in the USA
Lexington, KY
26 October 2015